Ninja Dual Zone
Air Fryer Cookbook
for Beginners UK

Quick & Mouthwatering Air Fryer
Recipes to Easily Prepare Daily Meals

Monica Sublett

All Rights Reserved.

The contents of this book may not be reproduced, copied or transmitted without the direct written permission of the author or publisher. Under no circumstances will the publisher or the author be held responsible or liable for any damage, compensation or pecuniary loss arising directly or indirectly from the information contained in this book.

Legal notice. This book is protected by copyright. It is intended for personal use only. You may not modify, distribute, sell, use, quote or paraphrase any part or content of this book without the consent of the author or publisher.

Notice Of Disclaimer.

Please note that the information in this document is intended for educational and entertainment purposes only. Every effort has been made to provide accurate, up-to-date, reliable and complete information. No warranty of any kind is declared or implied. The reader acknowledges that the author does not engage in the provision of legal, financial, medical or professional advice. The content in this book has been obtained from a variety of sources. Please consult a licensed professional before attempting any of the techniques described in this book. By reading this document, the reader agrees that in no event shall the author be liable for any direct or indirect damages, including but not limited to errors, omissions or inaccuracies, resulting from the use of the information in this document.

CONTENTS

BREAD AND BREAKFAST 10

Chili Hash Browns 10

Coconut Mini Tarts 10

Goat Cheese, Beet, And Kale Frittata 11

Colorful French Toast Sticks 11

Country Gravy 11

Bacon, Broccoli And Swiss Cheese Bread Pudding 12

Morning Apple Biscuits 12

Baked Eggs 12

Strawberry Toast 13

Cherry-apple Oatmeal Cups 13

Coffee Cake 13

Pumpkin Bread With Walnuts 14

Light Frittata 14

Crunchy French Toast Sticks 15

Granola 15

Orange Rolls 16

Favorite Blueberry Muffins 16

Morning Potato Cakes 16

Zucchini Hash Browns 17

Garlic-cheese Biscuits 17

Filled French Toast 18

APPETIZERS AND SNACKS 18

Cheese Wafers 18

Sweet-and-salty Pretzels 19

Parmesan Crackers 19

Dill Fried Pickles With Light Ranch Dip 19

Baked Ricotta With Lemon And Capers 20

Rich Clam Spread 21

Grilled Cheese Sandwich Deluxe 21

String Bean Fries 21

Cheesy Spinach Dip(2) 22

Cheesy Potato Canapés With Bacon 22

Fried Peaches 23	Garlic Parmesan Kale Chips 25
Homemade French Fries 23	Skinny Fries 26
Panko-breaded Onion Rings 23	Thai-style Crab Wontons 26
Crispy Wontons 24	Fried Dill Pickle Chips 27
Stuffed Mushrooms 25	Wrapped Smokies In Bacon 27
Roasted Jalapeño Salsa Verde 25	

POULTRY RECIPES 28

Mexican-inspired Chicken Breasts 28	Rich Turkey Burgers 32
Chicken Hand Pies 28	Buttered Turkey Breasts 33
Chicken Cordon Bleu 29	Nashville Hot Chicken 33
Guajillo Chile Chicken Meatballs 29	Simple Salsa Chicken Thighs 34
Mustardy Chicken Bites 29	Hawaiian Chicken 34
Easy Turkey Meatballs 30	Party Buffalo Chicken Drumettes 35
Berry-glazed Turkey Breast 30	Spinach And Feta Stuffed Chicken Breasts ... 35
Irresistible Cheesy Chicken Sticks 31	Peachy Chicken Chunks With Cherries 36
Chicken Strips 31	Spicy Black Bean Turkey Burgers With Cumin-avocado Spread 36
Kale & Rice Chicken Rolls 31	
Nacho Chicken Fries 32	Chicken Flautas 37

BEEF, PORK & LAMB RECIPES 37

Lamb Meatballs With Quick Tomato Sauce .. 37	Perfect Pork Chops 38

Chipotle Pork Meatballs 38

Delicious Juicy Pork Meatballs 39

Italian Sausage & Peppers............................... 39

Kielbasa Chunks With Pineapple & Peppers 40

Indonesian Pork Satay 40

Easy Tex-mex Chimichangas 40

Traditional Italian Beef Meatballs 41

Crispy Five-spice Pork Belly 41

Peppered Steak Bites.. 42

Argentinian Steak Asado Salad 42

Beefy Quesadillas 43

Balsamic London Broil..................................... 44

Sriracha Short Ribs 44

Chinese-style Lamb Chops............................. 44

Greek Pork Chops 45

Tender Steak With Salsa Verde 45

Albóndigas 45

Classic Salisbury Steak Burgers 46

Crunchy Fried Pork Loin Chops.................... 46

FISH AND SEAFOOD RECIPES 47

Beer-breaded Halibut Fish Tacos 47

Sardinas Fritas 48

Salmon Puttanesca En Papillotte With Zucchini 48

Panko-breaded Cod Fillets............................. 49

Garlicky Sea Bass With Root Veggies 49

Hot Calamari Rings.. 49

Lemon & Herb Crusted Salmon 50

Tilapia Al Pesto 50

Summer Sea Scallops 50

The Best Oysters Rockefeller 51

Tuna Nuggets In Hoisin Sauce.......................51

Chinese Fish Noodle Bowls............................ 52

Spiced Salmon Croquettes 52

Sweet & Spicy Swordfish Kebabs 53

Catfish Nuggets 53

Timeless Garlic-lemon Scallops 53

Beer-battered Cod 54

Kid's Flounder Fingers.................................... 54

Californian Tilapia 54

Maple Balsamic Glazed Salmon 55

Peppery Tilapia Roulade 55

VEGETARIAN RECIPES 56

Chive Potato Pierogi 56

Lentil Burritos With Cilantro Chutney 57

Cheddar Stuffed Portobellos With Salsa 57

Quick-to-make Quesadillas 57

Falafels 58

Mushroom Bolognese Casserole 58

Bengali Samosa With Mango Chutney 59

Pizza Margherita With Spinach 59

Falafel 59

Tortilla Pizza Margherita 60

Zucchini Tacos 60

Broccoli Cheddar Stuffed Potatoes 61

Basic Fried Tofu 61

Pizza Eggplant Rounds 62

Vegetarian Stuffed Bell Peppers 62

Mexican Twice Air-fried Sweet Potatoes 63

Cheddar-bean Flautas 63

Hearty Salad 63

Ricotta Veggie Potpie 64

Basil Green Beans 64

Italian-style Fried Cauliflower 65

VEGETABLE SIDE DISHES RECIPES 65

Herbed Baby Red Potato Hasselback 65

Lovely Mac'n'cheese 66

Buttery Stuffed Tomatoes 66

Broccoli Tots 67

Chicken Salad With Sunny Citrus Dressing .. 67

Acorn Squash Halves With Maple Butter Glaze 67

Butternut Medallions With Honey Butter And Sage 68

Steamboat Shrimp Salad 68

Pork Tenderloin Salad 69

Honey-mustard Asparagus Puffs	69	French Fries	72
Simple Roasted Sweet Potatoes	70	Stunning Apples & Onions	72
Pecorino Dill Muffins	70	Perfect Broccoli	72
Florentine Stuffed Tomatoes	71	Grits Casserole	73
Grits Again	71	Roasted Corn Salad	73
Truffle Vegetable Croquettes	71	Buttered Brussels Sprouts	74

SANDWICHES AND BURGERS RECIPES 74

Reuben Sandwiches	74	Inside-out Cheeseburgers	80
Thai-style Pork Sliders	75	Inside Out Cheeseburgers	80
Best-ever Roast Beef Sandwiches	75	Salmon Burgers	81
Eggplant Parmesan Subs	76	Dijon Thyme Burgers	81
Mexican Cheeseburgers	76	Chili Cheese Dogs	82
Crunchy Falafel Balls	77	Chicken Apple Brie Melt	83
Chicken Spiedies	77	Black Bean Veggie Burgers	83
Lamb Burgers	78	White Bean Veggie Burgers	84
Sausage And Pepper Heros	78	Chicken Club Sandwiches	84
Asian Glazed Meatballs	79	Chicken Gyros	85
Chicken Saltimbocca Sandwiches	79		

DESSERTS AND SWEETS 86

Coconut-custard Pie	86	Chocolate Soufflés	86

Fluffy Orange Cake 86

Baked Stuffed Pears 87

Holiday Peppermint Cake 87

Holiday Pear Crumble..................................... 88

Vegan Brownie Bites 88

Greek Pumpkin Cheesecake.......................... 88

Pumpkin Brownies... 89

Easy Bread Pudding 89

Honey Apple-pear Crisp................................. 90

Vanilla Butter Cake 90

Blueberry Crisp 91

Fruit Turnovers... 91

Cinnamon Canned Biscuit Donuts................. 91

Party S'mores 92

Cheese & Honey Stuffed Figs 92

Chocolate Cake... 92

Vanilla Cupcakes With Chocolate Chips 93

Chocolate Macaroons 93

Carrot Cake With Cream Cheese Icing.......... 94

INDEX 95

INTRODUCTION

Ninja Dual Zone Air Fryer Cookbook for Beginners UK

Are you ready to fully explore your Ninja Dual Zone Air Fryer and elevate your cooking to new heights?
Do you want to make meal prep easier while achieving amazing flavors and textures?

Absolutely! This book is designed to help you make the most of this extraordinary appliance. Inside, you'll find a collection of recipes that celebrate the best of British cuisine, reimagined for the air fryer. From classic comfort foods to contemporary favourites, our aim is to inspire you to experiment and explore.

In this fantastic cookbook, you will get:
Easy-to-find UK ingredients
Clear, concise cooking instructions
Tips for achieving better quality meals at home
Breakfast and Lunch Recipes
Vegetarian Recipes
Meat Recipes
Poultry Recipes
Fish and Seafood Recipes
Snack Recipes
Desserts
And So Much More...

Embrace the air frying revolution and elevate your cooking game. Secure your copy of the Ninja Dual Zone Air Fryer Cookbook today and embark on a culinary journey filled with quick, easy, and tasty dishes!

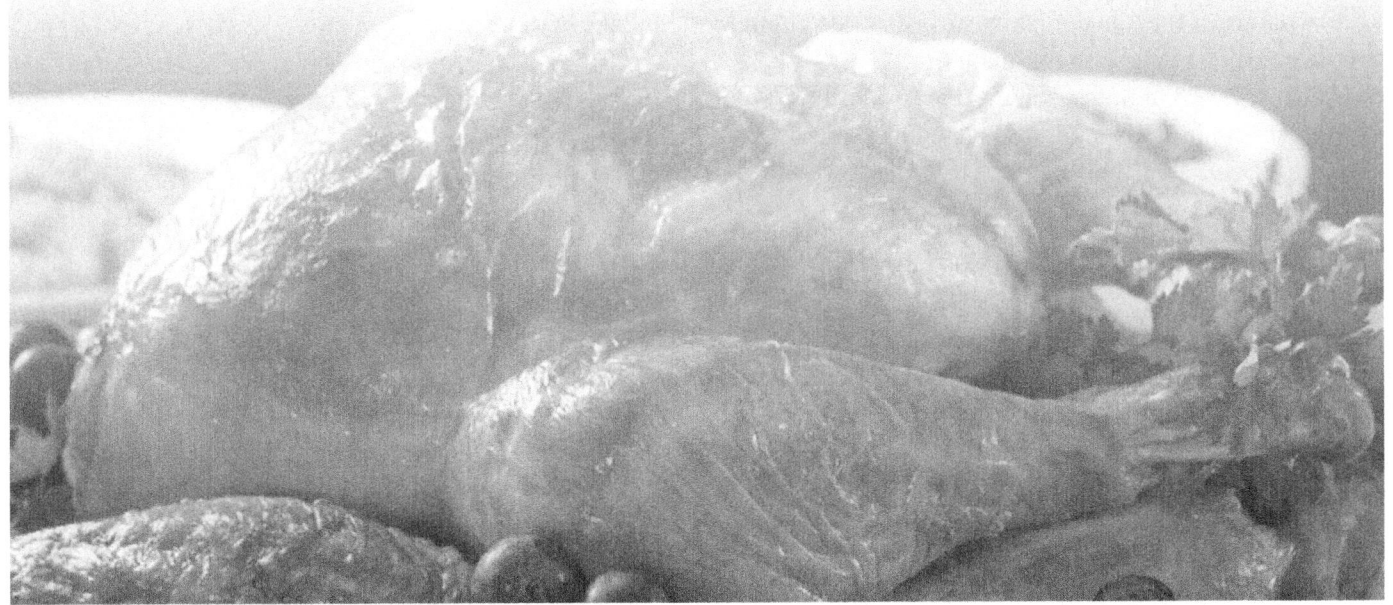

Bread And Breakfast

Chili Hash Browns

Servings: 4 | Prep Time: 10 Minutes | Cooking Time: 45 Minutes

Ingredients:

- 1 tablespoon ancho chili powder
- 1 tablespoon chipotle powder
- 2 teaspoons ground cumin
- 2 teaspoons smoked paprika
- 1 teaspoon garlic powder
- 1 teaspoon cayenne pepper
- Salt and pepper to taste
- 2 peeled russet potatoes, grated
- 2 tablespoons olive oil
- ⅓ cup chopped onion
- 3 garlic cloves, minced

Directions:

1. Preheat the air fryer to 200°C/400°F.
2. Combine chili powder, cumin, paprika, garlic powder, chipotle, cayenne, and black pepper in a small bowl, then pour into a glass jar with a lid and store in a cool, dry place.
3. Add the olive oil, onion, and garlic to a cake pan, put it in the air fryer, and Bake for 3 minutes.
4. Put the grated potatoes in a bowl and sprinkle with 2 teaspoons of the spice mixture, toss and add them to the cake pan along with the onion mix.
5. Bake for 20-23 minutes, stirring once or until the potatoes are crispy and golden. Season with salt and serve.

Variations & Ingredients Tips:

- Use different types of potatoes, such as sweet potatoes or Yukon Gold, for a variety of flavors and textures.
- Add some diced bell peppers or jalapeños to the hash browns for extra vegetables and heat.
- Serve the hash browns with a side of salsa or sour cream for a Mexican-inspired breakfast.

Per Serving: Calories: 220; Total Fat: 7g; Saturated Fat: 1g; Cholesterol: 0mg; Sodium: 50mg; Total Carbs: 36g; Fiber: 4g; Sugars: 2g; Protein: 5g

Coconut Mini Tarts

Servings: 2 | Prep Time: 10 Minutes | Cooking Time: 25 Minutes

Ingredients:

- ¼ cup almond butter
- 1 tablespoon coconut sugar
- 2 tablespoons coconut yogurt
- ½ cup oat flour
- 2 tablespoons strawberry jam

Directions:

1. Preheat air fryer to 180°C/350°F. Use 2 pieces of parchment paper, each 20 cm long. Draw a rectangle on one piece.
2. Beat the almond butter, coconut sugar, and coconut yogurt in a shallow bowl until well combined. Mix in oat flour until you get a dough.
3. Put the dough onto the undrawing paper and cover it with the other one, rectangle-side up. Using a rolling pin, roll out until you get a rectangle. Discard top paper.
4. Cut it into 4 equal rectangles. Spread on 2 rectangles, 1 tablespoon of strawberry jam each, then top with the remaining rectangles. Using a fork, press all edges to seal them.
5. Bake in the fryer for 8 minutes. Serve right away.

Variations & Ingredients Tips:

- Use different types of nut butter, such as cashew or walnut butter, for a variety of flavors.
- Add some shredded coconut or chopped nuts to the dough for extra texture.
- For a savory version, replace the strawberry jam with pesto or hummus.

Per Serving: Calories: 350; Total Fat: 24g; Saturated Fat: 5g; Cholesterol: 0mg; Sodium: 60mg; Total Carbs: 30g; Fiber: 4g; Sugars: 12g; Protein: 9g

Goat Cheese, Beet, And Kale Frittata

Servings: 6 | Prep Time: 10 Minutes | Cooking Time: 20 Minutes

Ingredients:

- 6 large eggs
- ½ teaspoon garlic powder
- ¼ teaspoon black pepper
- ¼ teaspoon salt
- 1 cup chopped kale
- 1 cup cooked and chopped red beets
- 85 g crumbled goat cheese

Directions:

1. Preheat the air fryer to 160°C/320°F.
2. In a medium bowl, whisk the eggs with the garlic powder, pepper, and salt. Mix in the kale, beets, and goat cheese.
3. Spray an oven-safe 18 cm springform pan with cooking spray. Pour the egg mixture into the pan and place it in the air fryer basket.
4. Cook for 20 minutes, or until the internal temperature reaches 63°C/145°F.
5. When the frittata is cooked, let it set for 5 minutes before removing from the pan.
6. Slice and serve immediately.

Variations & Ingredients Tips:

▶ Use Swiss chard, spinach or arugula instead of kale.
▶ Swap goat cheese for feta, ricotta or cream cheese.
▶ Add some sun-dried tomatoes, olives or roasted red peppers for Mediterranean flair.

Per Serving: Calories: 135; Total Fat: 9g; Saturated Fat: 4g; Cholesterol: 196mg; Sodium: 265mg; Total Carbs: 4g; Dietary Fiber: 1g; Total Sugars: 2g; Protein: 10g

Colorful French Toast Sticks

Servings: 4 | Prep Time: 10 Minutes | Cooking Time: 20 Minutes

Ingredients:

- 1 egg
- ⅓ cup whole milk
- Salt to taste
- ½ teaspoon ground cinnamon
- ½ teaspoon ground chia seeds
- 1 cup crushed pebbles
- 4 sandwich bread slices, each cut into 4 sticks
- ¼ cup honey

Directions:

1. Preheat air fryer at 190°C/375°F.
2. Whisk the egg, milk, salt, cinnamon and chia seeds in a bowl. In another bowl, add crushed cereal.
3. Dip breadsticks in the egg mixture, then dredge them in the cereal crumbs.
4. Place breadsticks in the greased frying basket and Air Fry for 5 minutes, flipping once.
5. Serve with honey as a dip.

Variations & Ingredients Tips:

▶ Use different types of bread, such as whole wheat or brioche, for a variety of flavors and textures.
▶ Add some vanilla extract or orange zest to the egg mixture for extra flavor.
▶ For a savory version, replace the cinnamon and honey with garlic powder and marinara sauce for dipping.

Per Serving: Calories: 240; Total Fat: 5g; Saturated Fat: 1.5g; Cholesterol: 50mg; Sodium: 330mg; Total Carbs: 43g; Fiber: 2g; Sugars: 18g; Protein: 7g

Country Gravy

Servings: 2 | Prep Time: 5 Minutes | Cooking Time: 7 Minutes

Ingredients:

- 115 g pork sausage, casings removed
- 1 tablespoon butter
- 2 tablespoons flour
- 2 cups whole milk
- ½ teaspoon salt
- Freshly ground black pepper
- 1 teaspoon fresh thyme leaves

Directions:

1. Preheat a saucepan over medium heat. Add and brown the sausage, crumbling it into small pieces as it cooks.
2. Add the butter and flour, stirring well to combine. Continue to cook for 2 minutes, stirring constantly.
3. Slowly pour in the milk, whisking as you do, and bring the mixture to a boil to thicken.
4. Season with salt and freshly ground black pepper, lower the heat and simmer until the sauce has thickened

to your desired consistency – about 5 minutes.
5. Stir in the fresh thyme, season to taste and serve hot.

Variations & Ingredients Tips:

- Use different types of sausage, such as turkey or chorizo, for a variety of flavors.
- Add some minced garlic or onion to the sausage for extra flavor.
- For a vegetarian version, replace the sausage with sautéed mushrooms or crumbled tempeh.

Per Serving: Calories: 400; Total Fat: 28g; Saturated Fat: 12g; Cholesterol: 85mg; Sodium: 1070mg; Total Carbs: 21g; Fiber: 0g; Sugars: 11g; Protein: 18g

Bacon, Broccoli And Swiss Cheese Bread Pudding

Servings: 2 | Prep Time: 15 Mins | Cooking Time: 48 Minutes

Ingredients:

- 227g thick cut bacon, cut into 0.6cm pieces
- 3 cups brioche bread or rolls, cut into 1.25cm cubes
- 3 eggs
- 1 cup milk
- ½ teaspoon salt
- Freshly ground black pepper
- 1 cup frozen broccoli florets, thawed and chopped
- 1½ cups grated Swiss cheese

Directions:

1. Preheat the air fryer to 205°C/400°F.
2. Air-fry the bacon for 6 minutes until crispy, shaking basket occasionally. Remove bacon to paper towel.
3. Air-fry the brioche cubes for 2 minutes to lightly toast. (Omit if bread is stale.)
4. Butter a 15-18cm cake pan. Combine all ingredients in a bowl and toss well. Transfer to buttered pan, cover with foil and refrigerate overnight or 8 hours.
5. Remove from fridge 1 hour before cooking to come to room temperature.
6. Preheat air fryer to 165°C/330°F. Transfer pan to air fryer basket using a foil sling. Air-fry covered for 20 minutes.
7. Remove foil and air-fry 20 more minutes until custard is set. Cover again if browning too quickly.

Variations & Ingredients Tips:

- Use ham or sausage instead of bacon.
- Add sautéed onions or bell peppers.
- Substitute cheddar or gruyere for the swiss.

Per Serving: Calories: 910; Total Fat: 53g; Saturated Fat: 24g; Cholesterol: 360mg; Sodium: 1615mg; Total Carbs: 52g; Dietary Fiber: 3g; Total Sugars: 7g; Protein: 51g

Morning Apple Biscuits

Servings: 6 | Prep Time: 5 Minutes | Cooking Time: 15 Minutes

Ingredients:

- 1 apple, grated
- 1 cup oat flour
- 2 tbsp honey
- 1/4 cup peanut butter
- 1/3 cup raisins
- 1/2 tsp ground cinnamon

Directions:

1. Preheat air fryer to 175°C/350°F.
2. Combine apple, flour, honey, peanut butter, raisins and cinnamon in a bowl.
3. Form into balls and flatten slightly.
4. Place on parchment paper in air fryer basket.
5. Bake for 9 minutes until lightly browned.
6. Serve warm.

Variations & Ingredients Tips:

- Use almond or cashew butter instead of peanut.
- Add chopped nuts or chocolate chips.
- Drizzle with maple syrup or dust with powdered sugar.

Per Serving: Calories: 140; Total Fat: 6g; Saturated Fat: 1g; Cholesterol: 0mg; Sodium: 45mg; 19g; Dietary Fiber: 3g; Sugars: 9g; Protein: 4g

Baked Eggs

Servings: 4 | Prep Time: 5 Minutes | Cooking Time: 6 Minutes

Ingredients:

- 4 large eggs
- ⅛ teaspoon black pepper
- ⅛ teaspoon salt

Directions:

1. Preheat the air fryer to 165°C/330°F. Place 4 silicone muffin liners into the air fryer basket.
2. Crack 1 egg at a time into each silicone muffin liner. Sprinkle with black pepper and salt.
3. Bake for 6 minutes. Remove and let cool 2 minutes prior to serving.

Variations & Ingredients Tips:

- Add shredded cheese, chopped herbs or cooked meats on top of eggs before baking.
- Use ramekins or oven-safe bowls instead of silicone liners.

Per Serving: Calories: 70; Total Fat: 5g; Saturated Fat: 1.5g; Cholesterol: 185mg; Sodium: 115mg; Total Carbs: 0g; Dietary Fiber: 0g; Total Sugars: 0g; Protein: 6g

Strawberry Toast

Servings: 4 | Prep Time: 5 Minutes | Cooking Time: 8 Minutes

Ingredients:

- 4 slices bread, 1.3-cm thick
- Butter-flavored cooking spray
- 1 cup sliced strawberries
- 1 teaspoon sugar

Directions:

1. Spray one side of bread slices with cooking spray.
2. Place slices spray-side down and top with strawberry slices.
3. Sprinkle sugar over strawberries.
4. Cook at 200°C/390°F for 8 minutes until bread is crisp and strawberries glazed.

Variations & Ingredients Tips:

- Use other fresh berries like blueberries or raspberries.
- Drizzle with honey or balsamic glaze before serving.
- Sprinkle with cinnamon or nutmeg in addition to sugar.

Per Serving: Calories: 96; Total Fat: 1g; Saturated Fat: 0g; Cholesterol: 0mg; Sodium: 144mg; Total Carbs: 20g; Dietary Fiber: 2g; Total Sugars: 5g; Protein: 3g

Cherry-apple Oatmeal Cups

Servings: 2 | Prep Time: 5 Minutes | Cooking Time: 20 Minutes

Ingredients:

- 2/3 cup rolled oats
- 1 cored apple, diced
- 4 pitted cherries, diced
- ½ tsp ground cinnamon
- ¾ cup milk

Directions:

1. Preheat air fryer to 177°C/350°F.
2. In a heatproof bowl, mix oats, apple, cherries and cinnamon.
3. Stir in milk.
4. Place bowl in air fryer basket and bake 6 minutes.
5. Stir well and bake 6 more minutes until fruit is soft.
6. Serve cooled.

Variations & Ingredients Tips:

- Use any variety of fresh or frozen berries.
- Substitute almond or oat milk for dairy milk.
- Top with nuts, seeds, honey or nut butter before serving.

Per Serving: Calories: 210; Total Fat: 3g; Saturated Fat: 1g; Cholesterol: 5mg; Sodium: 35mg; Total Carbs: 39g; Dietary Fiber: 5g; Total Sugars: 15g; Protein: 6g

Coffee Cake

Servings: 8 | Prep Time: 15 Minutes | Cooking Time: 35 Minutes

Ingredients:

- 4 tablespoons butter, melted and divided
- ⅓ cup cane sugar
- ¼ cup brown sugar
- 1 large egg
- 1 cup plus 6 teaspoons milk, divided
- 1 teaspoon vanilla extract
- 2 cups all-purpose flour
- 1½ teaspoons baking powder
- ¼ teaspoon salt
- 2 teaspoons ground cinnamon
- ⅓ cup chopped pecans
- ⅓ cup powdered sugar

Directions:

1. Preheat the air fryer to 165°C/325°F.
2. Using a hand mixer or stand mixer, in a medium bowl, cream together the butter, cane sugar, brown sugar, the egg, 1 cup of the milk, and the vanilla. Set aside.
3. In a small bowl, mix together the flour, baking powder, salt, and cinnamon. Slowly combine the dry ingredients into the wet. Fold in the pecans.
4. Liberally spray an 18 cm springform pan with cooking spray. Pour the batter into the pan and place in the air fryer basket.
5. Bake for 30 to 35 minutes. While the cake is baking, in a small bowl, add the powdered sugar and whisk together with the remaining 6 teaspoons of milk. Set aside.
6. When the cake is done baking, remove the pan from the basket and let cool on a wire rack. After 10 minutes, remove and invert the cake from pan. Drizzle with the powdered sugar glaze and serve.

Variations & Ingredients Tips:

- Substitute half of the all-purpose flour with whole wheat flour.
- Add 1 tsp ground nutmeg or allspice to the dry ingredients.
- Use walnuts or almonds instead of pecans.

Per Serving: Calories: 360; Total Fat: 15g; Saturated Fat: 7g; Cholesterol: 50mg; Sodium: 250mg; Total Carbohydrates: 52g; Dietary Fiber: 2g; Total Sugars: 28g; Protein: 5g

Pumpkin Bread With Walnuts

Servings: 6 | Prep Time: 10 Minutes | Cooking Time: 30 Minutes

Ingredients:

- 1/2 cup canned pumpkin puree
- 1 cup flour
- 1/2 tsp baking soda
- 1/2 cup granulated sugar
- 1 tsp pumpkin pie spice
- 1/4 tsp nutmeg
- 1/4 tsp salt
- 1 egg
- 1 tbsp vegetable oil
- 1 tbsp orange juice
- 1 tsp orange zest
- 1/4 cup crushed walnuts

Directions:

1. Preheat air fryer at 190°C/375°F.
2. In a bowl, mix flour, baking soda, sugar, spices, salt, pumpkin, egg, oil, orange juice, zest and walnuts.
3. Pour into a greased cake pan.
4. Place pan in air fryer basket and bake for 20 minutes.
5. Let cool 10 minutes before slicing and serving.

Variations & Ingredients Tips:

- Use pecans or a mix of nuts instead of walnuts.
- Drizzle with a powdered sugar glaze after baking.
- Add chocolate chips or raisins to the batter.

Per Serving: Calories: 200; Total Fat: 6g; Saturated Fat: 1g; Cholesterol: 25mg; Sodium: 195mg; Total Carbs: 35g; Dietary Fiber: 2g; Sugars: 18g; Protein: 3g

Light Frittata

Servings: 4 | Prep Time: 10 Minutes | Cooking Time: 25 Minutes

Ingredients:

- ½ red bell pepper, chopped
- 1 shallot, chopped
- 1 baby carrot, chopped
- 1 tablespoon olive oil
- 8 egg whites
- 79 ml milk
- 2 teaspoons grated Parmesan cheese

Directions:

1. Preheat air fryer to 175°C/350°F. Toss the red bell pepper, shallot, carrot, and olive oil in a baking pan. Put in the fryer and Bake for 4-6 minutes until the veggies are soft. Shake the basket once during cooking. Whisk the egg whites in a bowl until fluffy and stir in milk. Pour the mixture over the veggies. Toss some Parmesan cheese on top and put the pan back into the fryer. Bake for 4-6 minutes or until the frittata puffs. Serve and enjoy!

Variations & Ingredients Tips:

- Add some chopped spinach, kale or arugula for extra greens.
- Sprinkle with crumbled feta, goat cheese or shredded mozzarella.
- Top with sliced avocado, salsa or hot sauce before serving.

Per Serving: Calories: 86; Total Fat: 5g; Saturated Fat:

1g; Cholesterol: 3mg; Sodium: 106mg; Total Carbs: 3g; Dietary Fiber: 1g; Total Sugars: 2g; Protein: 8g

ed Fat: 5g; Cholesterol: 195mg; Sodium: 520mg; Total Carbs: 64g; Fiber: 3g; Sugars: 28g; Protein: 16g

Crunchy French Toast Sticks

Servings: 2 | Prep Time: 10 Minutes | Cooking Time: 9 Minutes

Ingredients:

- 2 eggs, beaten
- ¾ cup milk
- ½ teaspoon vanilla extract
- ½ teaspoon ground cinnamon
- 1½ cups crushed crunchy cinnamon cereal, or any cereal flakes
- 4 slices Texas Toast (or other bread that you can slice into 2.5 cm thick slices)
- Maple syrup, for serving
- Vegetable oil or melted butter

Directions:

1. Combine the eggs, milk, vanilla and cinnamon in a shallow bowl. Place the crushed cereal in a second shallow bowl.
2. Trim the crusts off the slices of bread and cut each slice into 3 sticks. Dip the sticks of bread into the egg mixture, turning them over to coat all sides. Let the bread sticks absorb the egg mixture for ten seconds or so, but don't let them get too wet. Roll the bread sticks in the cereal crumbs, pressing the cereal gently onto all sides so that it adheres to the bread.
3. Preheat the air fryer to 200°C/400°F.
4. Spray or brush the air fryer basket with oil or melted butter. Place the coated sticks in the basket. It's ok to stack a few on top of the others in the opposite direction.
5. Air-fry for 9 minutes. Turn the sticks over a couple of times during the cooking process so that the sticks crisp evenly.
6. Serve warm with the maple syrup or some berries.

Variations & Ingredients Tips:

- Use different types of cereal, such as cornflakes or granola, for a variety of flavors and textures.
- Add some orange zest or almond extract to the egg mixture for extra flavor.
- For a savory version, replace the cinnamon and maple syrup with garlic powder and marinara sauce for dipping.

Per Serving: Calories: 480; Total Fat: 19g; Saturat-

Granola

Servings: 2 | Preparation Time: 5 Minutes | Cooking Time: 40 Minutes

Ingredients:

- 1 cup rolled oats
- 3 tablespoons pure maple syrup
- 1 tablespoon sugar
- 1 tablespoon neutral-flavored oil, such as refined coconut, sunflower, or safflower
- 1/4 teaspoon sea salt
- 1/4 teaspoon ground cinnamon
- 1/4 teaspoon vanilla extract

Directions:

1. Insert the crisper plate into the basket and the basket into the unit. Preheat the unit by selecting BAKE, setting the temperature to 120°C/250°F, and set-ting the time to 3 minutes. Select START/STOP to begin.
2. In a medium bowl, stir together the oats, maple syrup, sugar, oil, salt, cinnamon, and vanilla until thoroughly combined. Transfer the granola to a 6-by-5-cm round baking pan.
3. Once the unit is preheated, place the pan into the basket.
4. Select BAKE, set the temperature to 120°C/250°F and set the time to 40 minutes. Select START/STOP to begin.
5. After 10 minutes, stir the granola well. Resume cooking, stirring the granola every 10 minutes, for a total of 40 minutes, or until the granola is lightly browned and mostly dry.
6. When the cooking is complete, place the granola on a plate to cool. It will become crisp as it cools. Store the completely cooled granola in an airtight container in a cool, dry place for 1 to 2 weeks.

Variations & Ingredients Tips:

- Use old-fashioned rolled oats for best texture.
- For clustered granola, avoid overstirring during baking.
- Let granola cool completely before storing for maximum crunchiness.

Per Serving: Calories: 330; Cholesterol: 0mg; Total Fat: 11g; Saturated Fat: 1.5g; Sodium: 155mg; Total Carbohydrates: 53g; Dietary Fiber: 4g; Total Sugars: 20g; Protein:

5g

Orange Rolls

Servings: 8 | Prep Time: 15 Minutes | Cooking Time: 10 Minutes

Ingredients:

- Parchment paper
- 85-g low-fat cream cheese
- 1 tbsp low-fat sour cream or plain yogurt
- 2 tsp sugar
- 1/4 tsp vanilla extract
- 1/4 tsp orange extract
- 1 (8 count) can organic crescent roll dough
- 1/4 cup chopped walnuts
- 1/4 cup dried cranberries
- 1/4 cup shredded sweetened coconut
- Butter-flavored cooking spray
- Orange Glaze:
- 1/2 cup powdered sugar
- 1 tbsp orange juice
- 1/4 tsp orange extract
- Dash of salt

Directions:

1. Cut parchment for air fryer basket and set aside.
2. Mix cream cheese, sour cream/yogurt, sugar, vanilla and orange extracts until smooth.
3. Preheat air fryer to 150°C/300°F.
4. Separate crescent dough into triangles. Spread cheese mix on each leaving 2.5cm border.
5. Sprinkle nuts, cranberries over cheese. Roll up from wide end.
6. Place on parchment, spray tops with cooking spray.
7. Air fry 4 rolls for 10 mins until golden.
8. Repeat with remaining rolls.
9. Make glaze and drizzle over warm rolls.

Variations & Ingredients Tips:

- Use different dried fruits or nuts.
- Substitute almond or lemon extract.
- Dust with powdered sugar instead of glaze.

Per Serving: Calories: 220; Total Fat: 12g; Saturated Fat: 4g; Cholesterol: 10mg; Sodium: 230mg; Total Carbs: 26g; Dietary Fiber: 1g; Sugars: 13g; Protein: 3g

Favorite Blueberry Muffins

Servings: 8 | Prep Time: 10 Minutes | Cooking Time: 25 Minutes

Ingredients:

- 1 cup all-purpose flour
- ½ teaspoon baking soda
- 1/3 cup granulated sugar
- ¼ teaspoon salt
- 1 tablespoon lemon juice
- 1 teaspoon lemon zest
- ¼ cup milk
- ½ teaspoon vanilla extract
- 1 egg
- 1 tablespoon vegetable oil
- ¼ cup halved blueberries
- 1 tablespoon powdered sugar

Directions:

1. Preheat air fryer at 190°C/375°F. Combine dry ingredients in a bowl. Mix 59 ml of fresh milk with 1 tsp of lemon juice and leave for 10 minutes. Put it in another bowl with the wet ingredients. Pour wet ingredients into dry ingredients and gently toss to combine. Fold in blueberries. Spoon mixture into 8 greased silicone cupcake liners and Bake them in the fryer for 6-8 minutes. Let cool onto a cooling rack. Serve right away sprinkled with powdered sugar.

Variations & Ingredients Tips:

- Use raspberries, blackberries or chopped strawberries instead of blueberries.
- Add some chopped nuts like almonds or pecans for crunch.
- Drizzle with a lemon glaze for extra tang and sweetness.

Per Serving: Calories: 143; Total Fat: 3g; Saturated Fat: 1g; Cholesterol: 24mg; Sodium: 155mg; Total Carbs: 27g; Dietary Fiber: 1g; Total Sugars: 14g; Protein: 3g

Morning Potato Cakes

Servings: 6 | Prep Time: 15 Minutes | Cooking Time: 50 Minutes

Ingredients:

- 4 Yukon Gold potatoes
- 2 cups kale, chopped

- 1 cup rice flour
- 1/4 cup cornstarch
- 3/4 cup milk
- 2 tbsp lemon juice
- 2 tsp dried rosemary
- 2 tsp shallot powder
- Salt and pepper to taste
- 1/2 tsp turmeric powder

Directions:

1. Preheat air fryer to 200°C/390°F.
2. Scrub and bake whole potatoes for 30 mins until soft.
3. Chop and mash potatoes. Mix with kale, flours, milk, lemon, spices, salt & pepper.
4. Form into 12 patties.
5. Grease air fryer basket and cook patties in batches for 10-12 mins, flipping once, until golden brown.
6. Serve warm.

Variations & Ingredients Tips:

- Add shredded cheese, bacon bits or chopped onions.
- Substitute cauliflower, zucchini or carrots for some of the potatoes.
- Use gluten-free flour if needed.

Per Serving: Calories: 140; Total Fat: 1g; Saturated Fat: 0g; Cholesterol: 1mg; Sodium: 70mg; Total Carbs: 30g; Dietary Fiber: 3g; Sugars: 2g; Protein: 3g

Zucchini Hash Browns

Servings: 4 | Prep Time: 8 Minutes | Cooking Time: 20 Minutes

Ingredients:

- 2 shredded zucchinis
- 2 tbsp nutritional yeast
- 1 tsp allspice
- 1 egg white

Directions:

1. Preheat air fryer to 200°C/400°F.
2. Combine zucchinis, nutritional yeast, allspice, and egg white in a bowl.
3. Make 4 patties out of the mixture.
4. Cut 4 pieces of parchment paper, put a patty on each, and fold in all sides to create a rectangle.
5. Using a spatula, flatten them and spread them out on the parchment.
6. Then unwrap each parchment and remove the hash browns onto the fryer and Air Fry for 12 minutes until golden brown and crispy, turning once.
7. Serve right away.

Variations & Ingredients Tips:

- Grate in carrots, onions or potatoes as well.
- Add shredded cheese or herbs like dill or parsley.
- Serve with salsa, sour cream or avocado on the side.

Per Serving: Calories: 41; Total Fat: 1g; Saturated Fat: 0g; Cholesterol: 0mg; Sodium: 34mg; Total Carbs: 6g; Dietary Fiber: 2g; Total Sugars: 3g; Protein: 4g

Garlic-cheese Biscuits

Servings: 8 | Prep Time: 10 Minutes | Cooking Time: 8 Minutes

Ingredients:

- 1 cup self-rising flour
- 1 teaspoon garlic powder
- 2 tablespoons butter, diced
- 57 g sharp Cheddar cheese, grated
- 118 ml milk
- cooking spray

Directions:

1. Preheat air fryer to 165°C/330°F.
2. Combine flour and garlic in a medium bowl and stir together.
3. Using a pastry blender or knives, cut butter into dry ingredients.
4. Stir in cheese.
5. Add milk and stir until stiff dough forms.
6. If dough is too sticky to handle, stir in 1 or 2 more tablespoons of self-rising flour before shaping. Biscuits should be firm enough to hold their shape. Otherwise, they'll stick to the air fryer basket.
7. Divide dough into 8 portions and shape into 5 cm biscuits about 2 cm thick.
8. Spray air fryer basket with nonstick cooking spray.
9. Place all 8 biscuits in basket and cook at 165°C/330°F for 8 minutes.

Variations & Ingredients Tips:

- Add some chopped chives, parsley or dill to the dough for herby flavor.
- Brush the tops with melted garlic butter after bak-

ing for extra richness.
- ▶ Serve with cream gravy, sausage or scrambled eggs for a hearty breakfast.

Per Serving: Calories: 128; Total Fat: 6g; Saturated Fat: 4g; Cholesterol: 17mg; Sodium: 323mg; Total Carbs: 14g; Dietary Fiber: 0g; Total Sugars: 1g; Protein: 4g

Filled French Toast

Servings: 4 | Prep Time: 15 Minutes | Cooking Time: 25 Minutes

Ingredients:

- 4 French bread slices
- 2 tablespoons blueberry jam
- 1/3 cup fresh blueberries
- 2 egg yolks
- 79 ml milk
- 1 tablespoon sugar
- ½ teaspoon vanilla extract
- 3 tablespoons sour cream

Directions:

1. Preheat the air fryer to 190°C/370°F. Cut a pocket into the side of each slice of bread. Don't cut all the way through. Combine the blueberry jam and blueberries and crush the blueberries into the jam with a fork. In a separate bowl, beat the egg yolks with milk, sugar, and vanilla until well combined. Smear some sour cream in the pocket of each bread slice and add the blueberry mix on top. Squeeze the edges of the bread to close the opening. Dip the bread in the egg mixture, soak for 3 minutes per side. In a single layer, put the bread in the greased frying basket and Air Fry for 5 minutes. Flip the bread and cook for 3-6 more minutes or until golden.

Variations & Ingredients Tips:

- ▶ Use strawberry, raspberry or apricot jam for different flavors.
- ▶ Stuff with cream cheese, mascarpone or ricotta mixed with sugar and cinnamon.
- ▶ Top with maple syrup, whipped cream and a dusting of powdered sugar.

Per Serving: Calories: 263; Total Fat: 9g; Saturated Fat: 4g; Cholesterol: 111mg; Sodium: 323mg; Total Carbs: 38g; Dietary Fiber: 2g; Total Sugars: 14g; Protein: 8g

Appetizers And Snacks

Cheese Wafers

Servings: 4 | Prep Time: 15 Minutes | Cooking Time: 6 Minutes Per Batch

Ingredients:

- 115 g sharp Cheddar cheese, grated
- ¼ cup butter
- ½ cup flour
- ¼ teaspoon salt
- ½ cup crisp rice cereal
- oil for misting or cooking spray

Directions:

1. Cream the butter and grated cheese together. You can do it by hand, but using a stand mixer is faster and easier.
2. Sift flour and salt together. Add it to the cheese mixture and mix until well blended.
3. Stir in cereal.
4. Place dough on wax paper and shape into a long roll about 2.5 cm in diameter. Wrap well with the wax paper and chill for at least 4 hours.
5. When ready to cook, preheat air fryer to 180°C/360°F.
6. Cut cheese roll into 6 mm slices.
7. Spray air fryer basket with oil or cooking spray and place slices in a single layer, close but not touching.
8. Cook for 6 minutes or until golden brown. When done, place them on paper towels to cool.

9. Repeat previous step to cook remaining cheese bites.

Variations & Ingredients Tips:

- Use different cheeses like Parmesan, Gruyère or Pepper Jack.
- Add some herbs or spices to the dough like rosemary, paprika or garlic powder.
- Shape the dough into coins, twists or other fun shapes.

Per Serving: Calories: 320; Total Fat: 24g; Saturated Fat: 15g; Cholesterol: 65mg; Sodium: 464mg; Total Carbs: 18g; Dietary Fiber: 1g; Total Sugars: 1g; Protein: 11g

Sweet-and-salty Pretzels

Servings: 4 | Prep Time: 5 Minutes | Cooking Time: 5 Minutes

Ingredients:

- 2 cups plain pretzel nuggets
- 1 tbsp Worcestershire sauce
- 2 tsp granulated white sugar
- 1 tsp mild smoked paprika
- ½ tsp garlic or onion powder

Directions:

1. Preheat the air fryer to 175°C/350°F. Put the pretzel nuggets, Worcestershire sauce, sugar, smoked paprika, and garlic or onion powder in a large bowl. Toss gently until the nuggets are well coated. When the machine is at temperature, pour the nuggets into the basket, spreading them into as close to a single layer as possible. Air-fry, shaking the basket three or four times to rearrange the nuggets, for 5 minutes, or until the nuggets are toasted and aromatic. Although the coating will darken, don't let it burn, especially if the machine's temperature is 180°C/360°F. Pour the nuggets onto a wire rack and gently spread them into one layer. (A rubber spatula does a good job.) Cool for 5 minutes before serving.

Variations & Ingredients Tips:

- Experiment with different spice blends like ranch seasoning, taco seasoning, or Italian herbs.
- Add a pinch of cayenne pepper or red pepper flakes for a spicy kick.
- Drizzle with melted chocolate or caramel for a sweet and salty treat.

Per Serving: Calories: 113; Total Fat: 1g; Saturated Fat: 0g; Sodium: 504mg; Total Carbohydrates: 24g; Dietary Fiber: 1g; Total Sugars: 3g; Protein: 3g

Parmesan Crackers

Servings: 6 | Prep Time: 5 Minutes | Cooking Time: 6 Minutes

Ingredients:

- 2 cups finely grated Parmesan cheese
- ¼ tsp paprika
- ¼ tsp garlic powder
- ½ tsp dried thyme
- 1 tbsp all-purpose flour

Directions:

1. Preheat the air fryer to 190°C/380°F. In a medium bowl, stir together the Parmesan, paprika, garlic powder, thyme, and flour. Line the air fryer basket with parchment paper. Using a tablespoon measuring tool, create 1-tablespoon mounds of seasoned cheese on the parchment paper, leaving 5 cm between the mounds to allow for spreading. Cook the crackers for 6 minutes. Allow the cheese to harden and cool before handling. Repeat in batches with the remaining cheese.

Variations & Ingredients Tips:

- Use different types of hard cheese like Asiago, Romano, or aged cheddar.
- Add finely chopped herbs like rosemary, basil, or oregano to the cheese mixture.
- For a spicy kick, add a pinch of cayenne pepper or red pepper flakes.

Per Serving: Calories: 138; Total Fat: 9g; Saturated Fat: 6g; Cholesterol: 29mg; Sodium: 529mg; Total Carbs: 2g; Dietary Fiber: 0g; Total Sugars: 0g; Protein: 11g

Dill Fried Pickles With Light Ranch Dip

Servings: 4 | Prep Time: 15 Minutes | Cooking Time: 8 Minutes

Ingredients:

- 4 to 6 large dill pickles, sliced in half or quartered lengthwise
- ½ cup all-purpose flour
- 2 eggs, lightly beaten

- 1 cup plain breadcrumbs
- 1 teaspoon salt
- ⅛ teaspoon cayenne pepper
- 2 tablespoons fresh dill leaves, dried well
- vegetable oil, in a spray bottle
- Light Ranch Dip
- ¼ cup reduced-fat mayonnaise
- ¼ cup buttermilk
- ¼ cup non-fat Greek yogurt
- 1 tablespoon chopped fresh chives
- 1 tablespoon chopped fresh parsley
- 1 tablespoon lemon juice
- salt and freshly ground black pepper

Directions:

1. Dry the dill pickle spears very well with a clean kitchen towel.
2. Set up a dredging station using three shallow dishes. Place the flour in the first shallow dish. Place the eggs into the second dish. Combine the breadcrumbs, salt, cayenne and fresh dill in a food processor and process until everything is combined and the crumbs are very fine. Place the crumb mixture in the third dish.
3. Preheat the air fryer to 200°C/400°F.
4. Coat the pickles by dredging them first in the flour, then the egg, and then the breadcrumbs, pressing the crumbs on gently with your hands. Set the coated pickles on a tray and spray them on all sides with vegetable oil.
5. Air-fry one layer of pickles at a time at 200°C/400°F for 8 minutes, turning them over halfway through the cooking process and spraying lightly again if necessary. The crumbs should be nicely browned on all sides.
6. While the pickles are air-frying, make the light ranch dip by mixing everything together in a bowl. Serve the pickles warm with the dip on the side.

Variations & Ingredients Tips:

- ▶ Use zucchini spears or green beans instead of pickles.
- ▶ Add some garlic powder, onion powder or smoked paprika to the breading.
- ▶ Serve with blue cheese dressing or spicy remoulade for dipping.

Per Serving: Calories: 245; Total Fat: 8g; Saturated Fat: 2g; Cholesterol: 98mg; Sodium: 1549mg; Total Carbs: 33g; Dietary Fiber: 2g; Total Sugars: 5g; Protein: 10g

Baked Ricotta With Lemon And Capers

Servings: 4 | Prep Time: 10 Minutes | Cooking Time: 10 Minutes

Ingredients:

- 18 cm pie dish or cake pan
- 1½ cups whole milk ricotta cheese
- zest of 1 lemon, plus more for garnish
- 1 teaspoon finely chopped fresh rosemary
- pinch crushed red pepper flakes
- 2 tablespoons capers, rinsed
- 2 tablespoons extra-virgin olive oil
- salt and freshly ground black pepper
- 1 tablespoon grated Parmesan cheese

Directions:

1. Preheat the air fryer to 190°C/380°F.
2. Combine the ricotta cheese, lemon zest, rosemary, red pepper flakes, capers, olive oil, salt and pepper in a bowl and whisk together well. Transfer the cheese mixture to an 18 cm pie dish and place the pie dish in the air fryer basket. You can use an aluminum foil sling to help with this by taking a long piece of aluminum foil, folding it in half lengthwise twice until it is roughly 66 cm by 7.5 cm. Place this under the pie dish and hold the ends of the foil to move the pie dish in and out of the air fryer basket. Tuck the ends of the foil beside the pie dish while it cooks in the air fryer.
3. Air-fry the ricotta at 190°C/380°F for 10 minutes, or until the top is nicely browned in spots.
4. Remove the pie dish from the air fryer and immediately sprinkle the Parmesan cheese on top. Drizzle with a little olive oil and add some freshly ground black pepper and lemon zest as garnish. Serve warm.

Variations & Ingredients Tips:

- ▶ Use goat cheese or feta instead of ricotta for a tangy flavor.
- ▶ Add some chopped sun-dried tomatoes or olives to the cheese mixture.
- ▶ Serve with crostini, pita chips or raw vegetables for dipping.

Per Serving: Calories: 271; Total Fat: 21g; Saturated Fat: 9g; Cholesterol: 47mg; Sodium: 325mg; Total Carbs: 5g; Dietary Fiber: 0g; Total Sugars: 1g; Protein: 14g

Rich Clam Spread

Servings: 6 | Prep Time: 15 Minutes | Cooking Time: 40 Minutes

Ingredients:

- 2 cans chopped clams in clam juice
- ⅓ cup panko bread crumbs
- 1 garlic clove, minced
- 1 tbsp olive oil
- 1 tbsp lemon juice
- ¼ tsp hot sauce
- 1 tsp Worcestershire sauce
- ½ tsp shallot powder
- ¼ tsp dried dill
- Salt and pepper to taste
- ½ tsp sweet paprika
- 4 tsp grated Parmesan cheese
- 2 celery stalks, chopped

Directions:

1. Completely drain one can of clams. Add them to a bowl along with the entire can of clams, breadcrumbs, garlic, olive oil, lemon juice, Worcestershire sauce, hot sauce, shallot powder, dill, pepper, salt, paprika, and 2 tbsp Parmesan. Combine well and set aside for 10 minutes. After that time, put the mixture in a greased baking dish. Preheat air fryer to 165°C/325°F. Put the dish in the air fryer and bake for 10 minutes. Sprinkle the remaining paprika and Parmesan, and continue to cook until golden brown on top, 8-10 minutes. Serve hot along with celery sticks.

Variations & Ingredients Tips:

- Add chopped bacon, sun-dried tomatoes, or artichoke hearts for extra flavor and texture.
- Serve with crackers, baguette slices, or pita chips for dipping.
- For a spicier version, increase the amount of hot sauce or add a pinch of cayenne pepper.

Per Serving: Calories: 99; Total Fat: 4g; Saturated Fat: 1g; Cholesterol: 16mg; Sodium: 312mg; Total Carbs: 8g; Dietary Fiber: 1g; Total Sugars: 1g; Protein: 7g

Grilled Cheese Sandwich Deluxe

Servings: 4 | Prep Time: 10 Minutes | Cooking Time: 6 Minutes

Ingredients:

- 225 g Brie
- 8 slices oat nut bread
- 1 large ripe pear, cored and cut into 13 mm thick slices
- 2 tablespoons butter, melted

Directions:

1. Spread a quarter of the Brie on each of four slices of bread.
2. Top Brie with thick slices of pear, then the remaining 4 slices of bread.
3. Lightly brush both sides of each sandwich with melted butter.
4. Cooking 2 at a time, place sandwiches in air fryer basket and cook at 180°C/360°F for 6 minutes or until cheese melts and outside looks golden brown.

Variations & Ingredients Tips:

- Use apples, figs or apricots instead of pears.
- Add some prosciutto, turkey or smoked salmon to the filling.
- Sprinkle the outside of the sandwiches with cinnamon sugar before cooking.

Per Serving: Calories: 431; Total Fat: 23g; Saturated Fat: 13g; Cholesterol: 67mg; Sodium: 562mg; Total Carbs: 44g; Dietary Fiber: 4g; Total Sugars: 11g; Protein: 14g

String Bean Fries

Servings: 4 | Prep Time: 15 Minutes | Cooking Time: 6 Minutes

Ingredients:

- 225 g fresh string beans
- 2 eggs
- 4 tsp water
- ½ cup white flour
- ½ cup breadcrumbs
- ¼ tsp salt
- ¼ tsp ground black pepper
- ¼ tsp dry mustard (optional)
- oil for misting or cooking spray

Directions:

1. Preheat air fryer to 180°C/360°F. Trim stem ends from string beans, wash, and pat dry. In a shallow dish, beat eggs and water together until well blended. Place flour

in a second shallow dish. In a third shallow dish, stir together the breadcrumbs, salt, pepper, and dry mustard if using. Dip each string bean in egg mixture, flour, egg mixture again, then breadcrumbs. When you finish coating all the string beans, open air fryer and place them in basket. Cook for 3 minutes. Stop and mist string beans with oil or cooking spray. Cook for 3 more minutes or until string beans are crispy and nicely browned.

Variations & Ingredients Tips:

- Use panko breadcrumbs or crushed potato chips for a crunchier coating.
- Add grated Parmesan cheese, garlic powder, or smoked paprika to the breadcrumb mixture for extra flavor.
- Serve with ranch dressing, garlic aioli, or marinara sauce for dipping.

Per Serving: Calories: 174; Total Fat: 4g; Saturated Fat: 1g; Cholesterol: 93mg; Sodium: 293mg; Total Carbohydrates: 27g; Dietary Fiber: 3g; Total Sugars: 3g; Protein: 8g

Cheesy Spinach Dip(2)

Servings: 8 | Prep Time: 15 Minutes | Cooking Time: 30 Minutes

Ingredients:

- 1 can refrigerated biscuit dough
- 115 g cream cheese, softened
- ¼ cup mayonnaise
- 1 cup spinach
- 60 g cooked bacon, crumbled
- 2 scallions, chopped
- 2 cups grated Fontina cheese
- 1 cup grated cheddar
- ½ tsp garlic powder

Directions:

1. Preheat the air fryer to 175°C/350°F. Divide the dough into 8 biscuits and press each one into and up the sides of the silicone muffin cup, then set aside. Combine the cream cheese and mayonnaise and beat until smooth. Stir in the spinach, bacon, scallions, 1 cup of cheddar cheese and garlic powder. Then divide the mixture between the muffin cups. Put them in the basket and top each with 1 tbsp of Fontina cheese. Bake for 8-13 minutes or until the dough is golden and the filling is hot and bubbling. Remove from the air fryer and cool on a wire rack. Serve.

Variations & Ingredients Tips:

- Add some diced jalapeños or hot sauce for a spicy kick.
- Use Swiss, Gruyère or Gouda cheese instead of Fontina.
- Garnish with chopped tomatoes, red onions or fresh herbs.

Per Serving: Calories: 355; Total Fat: 25g; Saturated Fat: 13g; Cholesterol: 61mg; Sodium: 657mg; Total Carbs: 19g; Dietary Fiber: 1g; Total Sugars: 3g; Protein: 15g

Cheesy Potato Canapés With Bacon

Servings: 4 | Prep Time: 15 Minutes | Cooking Time: 35 Minutes

Ingredients:

- 4 bacon slices
- 4 russet potatoes, sliced
- 1 tbsp olive oil
- 1 tsp mustard powder
- Salt and pepper to taste
- 1 cup grated cheddar
- 2 tsp chopped chives
- 2 tsp chopped scallions

Directions:

1. Cook bacon in a skillet for 5 minutes over medium heat. Drain on a paper towel and crumble. Set aside. Add the potatoes to a large bowl and coat them with olive oil, mustard powder, salt and pepper.
2. Preheat air fryer to 200°C/400°F. Place the potatoes in the greased frying basket. Air Fry for 10 minutes. Shake the basket and cook for another 5-8 minutes or until potatoes are cooked through and edges are crisp. Transfer the potato bites to a serving dish. Serve warm topped with cheese, bacon, chives, and scallions.

Variations & Ingredients Tips:

- Use sweet potatoes or zucchini slices instead of russet potatoes.
- Top with blue cheese, goat cheese or feta for a tangy twist.
- Drizzle with ranch dressing or sour cream before serving.

Per Serving: Calories: 338; Total Fat: 19g; Saturated

Fat: 8g; Cholesterol: 45mg; Sodium: 410mg; Total Carbs: 30g; Dietary Fiber: 3g; Total Sugars: 2g; Protein: 14g

Fried Peaches

Servings: 4 | Prep Time: 15 Minutes | Cooking Time: 8 Minutes

Ingredients:

- 2 egg whites
- 1 tablespoon water
- ¼ cup sliced almonds
- 2 tablespoons brown sugar
- ½ teaspoon almond extract
- 1 cup crisp rice cereal
- 2 medium, very firm peaches, peeled and pitted
- ¼ cup cornstarch
- oil for misting or cooking spray

Directions:

1. Preheat air fryer to 200°C/390°F.
2. Beat together egg whites and water in a shallow dish.
3. In a food processor, combine the almonds, brown sugar, and almond extract. Process until ingredients combine well and the nuts are finely chopped.
4. Add cereal and pulse just until cereal crushes. Pour crumb mixture into a shallow dish or onto a plate.
5. Cut each peach into eighths and place in a plastic bag or container with lid. Add cornstarch, seal, and shake to coat.
6. Remove peach slices from bag or container, tapping them hard to shake off the excess cornstarch. Dip in egg wash and roll in crumbs. Spray with oil.
7. Place in air fryer basket and cook for 5 minutes. Shake basket, separate any that have stuck together, and spritz a little oil on any spots that aren't browning.
8. Cook for 3 minutes longer, until golden brown and crispy.

Variations & Ingredients Tips:

- Use nectarines, apricots or plums instead of peaches.
- Add some cinnamon, nutmeg or cardamom to the crumb mixture.
- Serve with vanilla ice cream, whipped cream or caramel sauce for dipping.

Per Serving: Calories: 172; Total Fat: 5g; Saturated Fat: 1g; Cholesterol: 0mg; Sodium: 76mg; Total Carbs: 30g; Dietary Fiber: 3g; Total Sugars: 17g; Protein: 4g

Homemade French Fries

Servings: 2 | Prep Time: 15 Minutes | Cooking Time: 25 Minutes

Ingredients:

- 2 to 3 russet potatoes, peeled and cut into 13 mm sticks
- 2 to 3 teaspoons olive or vegetable oil
- salt

Directions:

1. Bring a large saucepan of salted water to a boil on the stovetop while you peel and cut the potatoes. Blanch the potatoes in the boiling salted water for 4 minutes while you Preheat the air fryer to 200°C/400°F. Strain the potatoes and rinse them with cold water. Dry them well with a clean kitchen towel.
2. Toss the dried potato sticks gently with the oil and place them in the air fryer basket. Air-fry for 25 minutes, shaking the basket a few times while the fries cook to help them brown evenly. Season the fries with salt mid-way through cooking and serve them warm with tomato ketchup, Sriracha mayonnaise or a mix of lemon zest, Parmesan cheese and parsley.

Variations & Ingredients Tips:

- Use sweet potatoes, parsnips or turnips instead of russets.
- Season the fries with garlic powder, onion powder or Old Bay seasoning.
- Serve with malt vinegar, truffle aioli or chimichurri sauce for dipping.

Per Serving: Calories: 266; Total Fat: 7g; Saturated Fat: 1g; Cholesterol: 0mg; Sodium: 12mg; Total Carbs: 48g; Dietary Fiber: 5g; Total Sugars: 2g; Protein: 5g

Panko-breaded Onion Rings

Servings: 4 | Prep Time: 15 Minutes | Cooking Time: 12 Minutes

Ingredients:

- 1 large sweet onion, cut into 1.3-cm slices and rings separated
- 2 cups ice water
- ½ cup all-purpose flour
- 1 tsp paprika
- 1 tsp salt

23

- ½ tsp black pepper
- ½ tsp garlic powder
- ¼ tsp onion powder
- 1 egg, whisked
- 2 tbsp milk
- 1 cup breadcrumbs

Directions:

1. Preheat the air fryer to 200°C/400°F. In a large bowl, soak the onion rings in the water for 5 minutes. Drain and pat dry with a towel. In a medium bowl, place the flour, paprika, salt, pepper, garlic powder, and onion powder. In a second bowl, whisk together the egg and milk. In a third bowl, place the breadcrumbs. To bread the onion rings, dip them first into the flour mixture, then into the egg mixture (shaking off the excess), and then into the breadcrumbs. Place the coated onion rings onto a plate while you bread all the rings. Place the onion rings into the air fryer basket in a single layer, sometimes nesting smaller rings into larger rings. Spray with cooking spray. Cook for 3 minutes, turn the rings over, and spray with more cooking spray. Cook for another 3 to 5 minutes. Cook the rings in batches; you may need to do 2 or 3 batches, depending on the size of your air fryer.

Variations & Ingredients Tips:

- For a spicy twist, add cayenne pepper or chili powder to the flour mixture.
- Use panko breadcrumbs for an extra crispy texture.
- Serve with your favorite dipping sauce like ranch, honey mustard, or BBQ sauce.

Per Serving: Calories: 193; Total Fat: 3g; Saturated Fat: 1g; Cholesterol: 47mg; Sodium: 764mg; Total Carbs: 35g; Dietary Fiber: 2g; Total Sugars: 4g; Protein: 7g

Crispy Wontons

Servings: 8 | Prep Time: 30 Minutes | Cooking Time: 10 Minutes

Ingredients:

- ½ cup refried beans
- 3 tablespoons salsa
- ¼ cup canned artichoke hearts, drained and patted dry
- ¼ cup frozen spinach, defrosted and squeezed dry
- 60 g cream cheese
- 1½ teaspoons dried oregano, divided
- ¼ teaspoon garlic powder
- ¼ teaspoon onion powder
- ½ teaspoon salt
- ¼ cup chopped pepperoni
- ¼ cup grated mozzarella cheese
- 1 tablespoon grated Parmesan
- 60 g cream cheese
- ½ teaspoon dried oregano
- 32 wontons
- 1 cup water

Directions:

1. Preheat the air fryer to 190°C/370°F.
2. In a medium bowl, mix together the refried beans and salsa.
3. In a second medium bowl, mix together the artichoke hearts, spinach, cream cheese, oregano, garlic powder, onion powder, and salt.
4. In a third medium bowl, mix together the pepperoni, mozzarella cheese, Parmesan cheese, cream cheese, and the remaining ½ teaspoon of oregano.
5. Get a towel lightly damp with water and ring it out. While working with the wontons, leave the unfilled wontons under the damp towel so they don't dry out.
6. Working with 8 wontons at a time, place 2 teaspoons of one of the fillings into the center of the wonton, rotating among the different fillings (one filling per wonton). Working one at a time, use a pastry brush, dip the pastry brush into the water, and brush the edges of the dough with the water. Fold the dough in half to form a triangle and set aside. Continue until 8 wontons are formed. Spray the wontons with cooking spray and cover with a dry towel. Repeat until all 32 wontons have been filled.
7. Place the wontons into the air fryer basket, leaving space between the wontons, and cook for 5 minutes. Turn over and check for brownness, and then cook for another 5 minutes.

Variations & Ingredients Tips:

- Use ground beef, sausage or shrimp instead of pepperoni.
- Add some diced jalapeños, green chiles or sriracha for spice.
- Serve with soy sauce, sweet chili sauce or duck sauce for dipping.

Per Serving: Calories: 193; Total Fat: 9g; Saturated Fat: 5g; Cholesterol: 30mg; Sodium: 587mg; Total Carbs: 21g; Dietary Fiber: 2g; Total Sugars: 1g; Protein: 7g

Stuffed Mushrooms

Servings: 10 | Prep Time: 10 Minutes | Cooking Time: 8 Minutes

Ingredients:

- 225 g white mushroom caps, stems removed
- salt
- 6 fresh mozzarella cheese balls
- ground dried thyme
- ¼ roasted red pepper cut into small pieces (about 1.3 cm)

Directions:

1. Sprinkle inside of mushroom caps with salt to taste. Cut mozzarella balls in half. Stuff each cap with half a mozzarella cheese ball. Sprinkle very lightly with thyme. Top each mushroom with a small strip of roasted red pepper, lightly pressing it into the cheese. Cook at 200°C/390°F for 8 minutes or longer if you prefer softer mushrooms.

Variations & Ingredients Tips:

- Use goat cheese, feta, or ricotta instead of mozzarella for a tangy flavor.
- Add a pinch of red pepper flakes, garlic powder, or Italian seasoning to the cheese for extra zing.
- Garnish with fresh basil leaves, pine nuts, or a drizzle of balsamic glaze before serving.

Per Serving: Calories: 74; Total Fat: 5g; Saturated Fat: 3g; Cholesterol: 17mg; Sodium: 122mg; Total Carbohydrates: 2g; Dietary Fiber: 0g; Total Sugars: 1g; Protein: 5g

Roasted Jalapeño Salsa Verde

Servings: 4 | Prep Time: 10 Minutes | Cooking Time: 20 Minutes

Ingredients:

- 340 g fresh tomatillos, husked
- 1 jalapeño, stem removed
- 4 green onions, sliced
- 3 garlic cloves, peeled
- ½ tsp salt
- 1 tsp lime juice
- ¼ tsp apple cider vinegar
- ¼ cup cilantro leaves

Directions:

1. Preheat air fryer to 200°C/400°F. Add tomatillos and jalapeño to the frying basket and bake for 5 minutes. Put in green onions and garlic and bake for 5 more minutes. Transfer it into a food processor along with salt, lime juice, vinegar and cilantro and blend until the sauce is finely chopped. Pour it into a small sealable container and refrigerate it until ready to use up to five days.

Variations & Ingredients Tips:

- Use serrano peppers or habaneros instead of jalapeños for a spicier salsa.
- Add avocado for a creamier texture and flavor.
- Grill the vegetables instead of air frying for a smokier taste.

Per Serving: Calories: 41; Total Fat: 1g; Saturated Fat: 0g; Cholesterol: 0mg; Sodium: 296mg; Total Carbs: 8g; Dietary Fiber: 2g; Total Sugars: 4g; Protein: 1g

Garlic Parmesan Kale Chips

Servings: 2 | Prep Time: 5 Minutes | Cooking Time: 6 Minutes

Ingredients:

- 16 large kale leaves, washed and thick stems removed
- 1 tablespoon avocado oil
- ½ teaspoon garlic powder
- 1 teaspoon soy sauce or tamari
- ¼ cup grated Parmesan cheese

Directions:

1. Preheat the air fryer to 190°C/370°F.
2. Make a stack of kale leaves and cut them into 4 pieces.
3. Place the kale pieces into a large bowl. Drizzle the avocado oil onto the kale and rub to coat. Add the garlic powder, soy sauce or tamari, and cheese, tossing to coat.
4. Pour the chips into the air fryer basket and cook for 3 minutes, shake the basket, and cook another 3 minutes, checking for crispness every minute. When done cooking, pour the kale chips onto paper towels and cool at least 5 minutes before serving.

Variations & Ingredients Tips:

- Use spinach, Swiss chard or collard greens instead of kale.

- Add some smoked paprika, nutritional yeast or lemon zest for extra flavor.
- Store leftovers in an airtight container at room temperature for up to 3 days.

Per Serving: Calories: 160; Total Fat: 13g; Saturated Fat: 3g; Cholesterol: 11mg; Sodium: 520mg; Total Carbs: 7g; Dietary Fiber: 2g; Total Sugars: 1g; Protein: 6g

Skinny Fries

Servings: 2 | Prep Time: 20 Minutes | Cooking Time: 15 Minutes

Ingredients:

- 2 to 3 russet potatoes, peeled and cut into 6 mm sticks
- 2 to 3 teaspoons olive or vegetable oil
- Salt

Directions:

1. Cut the potatoes into 6 mm strips. (A mandolin with a julienne blade is really helpful here.) Rinse the potatoes with cold water several times and let them soak in cold water for at least 10 minutes or as long as overnight.
2. Preheat the air fryer to 190°C/380°F.
3. Drain and dry the potato sticks really well, using a clean kitchen towel. Toss the fries with the oil in a bowl and then air-fry the fries in two batches at 190°C/380°F for 15 minutes, shaking the basket a couple of times while they cook.
4. Add the first batch of French fries back into the air fryer basket with the finishing batch and let everything warm through for a few minutes. As soon as the fries are done, season them with salt and transfer to a plate or basket. Serve them warm with ketchup or your favorite dip.

Variations & Ingredients Tips:

- Use sweet potatoes instead of russet potatoes for a different flavor and nutritional profile.
- Season the fries with garlic powder, onion powder, paprika, or your favorite spice blend before cooking.
- Serve the fries with aioli, ranch dressing, or truffle mayo for a gourmet twist.

Per Serving: Calories: 180; Total Fat: 5g; Saturated Fat: 1g; Cholesterol: 0mg; Sodium: 10mg; Total Carbs: 31g; Fiber: 3g; Sugars: 1g; Protein: 4g

Thai-style Crab Wontons

Servings: 4 | Prep Time: 20 Minutes | Cooking Time: 20 Minutes

Ingredients:

- 115 g cottage cheese, softened
- 70 g lump crabmeat
- 2 scallions, chopped
- 2 garlic cloves, minced
- 2 tsp tamari sauce
- 12 wonton wrappers
- 1 egg white, beaten
- 5 tbsp Thai sweet chili sauce

Directions:

1. Using a fork, mix together cottage cheese, crabmeat, scallions, garlic, and tamari sauce in a bowl. Set it near your workspace along with a small bowl of water. Place one wonton wrapper on a clean surface. The points should be facing so that it looks like a diamond. Put 1 level tbsp of the crab and cheese mix onto the center of the wonton wrapper. Dip your finger into the water and run the moist finger along the edges of the wrapper. Fold one corner of the wrapper to the opposite side and make a triangle. From the center out, press out any air and seal the edges. Continue this process until all of the wontons have been filled and sealed. Brush both sides of the wontons with beaten egg white. Preheat air fryer to 170°C/340°F. Place the wontons on the bottom of the greased frying basket in a single layer. Bake for 8 minutes, flipping the wontons once until golden brown and crispy. Serve hot and enjoy!

Variations & Ingredients Tips:

- Substitute crab with cooked, shredded chicken, pork, or shrimp for a different filling.
- Add finely chopped water chestnuts, bamboo shoots, or mushrooms for extra crunch and flavor.
- Serve with hoisin sauce, soy sauce, or plum sauce for dipping.

Per Serving: Calories: 204; Total Fat: 4g; Saturated Fat: 1g; Cholesterol: 37mg; Sodium: 648mg; Total Carbohydrates: 29g; Dietary Fiber: 1g; Total Sugars: 10g; Protein: 12g

Fried Dill Pickle Chips

Servings: 4 | Prep Time: 15 Minutes | Cooking Time: 12 Minutes

Ingredients:

- 1 cup All-purpose flour or tapioca flour
- 1 Large egg white(s)
- 1 tablespoon Brine from a jar of dill pickles
- 1 cup Seasoned Italian-style dried bread crumbs (gluten-free, if a concern)
- 2 Large dill pickle(s) (20 to 25 cm long), cut into 13 mm thick rounds
- Vegetable oil spray

Directions:

1. Preheat the air fryer to 200°C/400°F.
2. Set up and fill three shallow soup plates or small pie plates on your counter: one for the flour, one for the egg white(s) whisked with the pickle brine, and one for the bread crumbs.
3. Set a pickle round in the flour and turn it to coat all sides, even the edge. Gently shake off the excess flour, then dip the round into the egg-white mixture and turn to coat both sides and the edge. Let any excess egg white mixture slip back into the rest, then set the round in the bread crumbs and turn it to coat both sides as well as the edge. Set aside on a cutting board and soldier on, dipping and coating the remaining rounds. Lightly coat the coated rounds on both sides with vegetable oil spray.
4. Set the pickle rounds in the basket in one layer. Air-fry undisturbed for 7 minutes, or until golden brown and crunchy. Cool in the basket for a few minutes before using kitchen tongs to transfer the (still hot) rounds to a serving platter.

Variations & Ingredients Tips:

- Use zucchini, eggplant or green tomato slices instead of pickles.
- Add some smoked paprika, cayenne pepper or ranch seasoning to the breading.
- Serve with ranch dressing, blue cheese dip or spicy mayo for dipping.

Per Serving: Calories: 239; Total Fat: 2g; Saturated Fat: 0g; Cholesterol: 0mg; Sodium: 1625mg; Total Carbs: 47g; Dietary Fiber: 3g; Total Sugars: 4g; Protein: 8g

Wrapped Smokies In Bacon

Servings: 4 | Prep Time: 5 Minutes | Cooking Time: 15 Minutes

Ingredients:

- 8 small smokies
- 8 bacon strips, sliced
- Salt and pepper to taste

Directions:

1. Preheat air fryer to 175°C/350°F. Wrap the bacon slices around smokies. Arrange the rolls, seam side down, on the greased frying basket. Sprinkle with salt and pepper and air fry for 5-8 minutes, turning once until the bacon is crisp and juicy around them. Serve and enjoy!

Variations & Ingredients Tips:

- Use turkey bacon, prosciutto, or pancetta instead of regular bacon for a twist.
- Brush the wrapped smokies with maple syrup, honey, or brown sugar before cooking for a sweet and savory combo.
- Serve with mustard, ketchup, or BBQ sauce for dipping.

Per Serving: Calories: 186; Total Fat: 15g; Saturated Fat: 5g; Cholesterol: 32mg; Sodium: 578mg; Total Carbohydrates: 1g; Dietary Fiber: 0g; Total Sugars: 0g; Protein: 9g

Poultry Recipes

Mexican-inspired Chicken Breasts

Servings: 4 | Prep Time: 10 Minutes | Cooking Time: 20 Minutes

Ingredients:

- 1/8 tsp crushed red pepper flakes
- 1 red pepper, deseeded and diced
- Salt to taste
- 4 chicken breasts
- 3/4 tsp garlic powder
- 1/2 tsp onion powder
- 1/2 tsp ground cumin
- 1/2 tsp ancho chile powder
- 1/2 tsp sweet paprika
- 1/2 tsp Mexican oregano
- 1 tomato, chopped
- 1/2 diced red onion
- 3 tbsp fresh lime juice
- 285g avocado, diced
- 1 tbsp chopped cilantro

Directions:

1. Preheat air fryer to 190°C/380°F.
2. Stir together salt, garlic and onion powder, cumin, ancho chili powder, paprika, Mexican oregano, and pepper flakes in a bowl.
3. Spray the chicken with cooking oil and rub with the spice mix. Air Fry the chicken for 10 minutes, flipping once until browned and fully cooked. Repeat for all of the chicken.
4. Mix the onion and lime juice in a bowl. Fold in the avocado, cilantro, red pepper, salt, and tomato and coat gently.
5. To serve, top the chicken with guacamole salsa.

Variations & Ingredients Tips:

- Use boneless, skinless chicken thighs for juicier meat.
- Add some crumbled cotija or feta cheese on top.
- Serve sliced over a bed of rice and black beans.

Per Serving: Calories: 400; Total Fat: 22g; Saturated Fat: 4g; Cholesterol: 145mg; Sodium: 420mg; Total Carbs: 10g; Dietary Fiber: 6g; Total Sugars: 3g; Protein: 44g

Chicken Hand Pies

Servings: 8 | Prep Time: 20 Minutes | Cooking Time: 10 Minutes Per Batch

Ingredients:

- 3/4 cup chicken broth
- 3/4 cup frozen mixed peas and carrots
- 1 cup cooked chicken, chopped
- 1 tablespoon cornstarch
- 1 tablespoon milk
- Salt and pepper
- 1 8-count can organic flaky biscuits
- Oil for misting or cooking spray

Directions:

1. In a saucepan, bring broth to a boil. Add peas, carrots and chicken.
2. Mix cornstarch and milk, then stir into broth mixture until thickened.
3. Remove from heat, season with salt and pepper, and let cool slightly.
4. Separate biscuits into 16 rounds, flattening each slightly.
5. Place filling on 8 biscuit rounds. Top with remaining rounds and crimp edges sealed.
6. Mist both sides with oil or cooking spray.
7. Air fry in batches at 165°C/330°F for 10 minutes until golden brown.

Variations & Ingredients Tips:

- Use rotisserie or leftover chicken.
- Add diced potatoes, celery or onions to the filling.
- Brush with egg wash before cooking for a shiny finish.

Per Serving (2 hand pies): Calories: 312; Total Fat: 11g; Saturated Fat: 3g; Cholesterol: 38mg; Sodium: 779mg; Total Carbs: 41g; Dietary Fiber: 3g; Total Sugars:

4g; Protein: 13g

Chicken Cordon Bleu

Servings: 2 | Prep Time: 15 Minutes | Cooking Time: 16 Minutes

Ingredients:

- 2 boneless, skinless chicken breasts
- ¼ teaspoon salt
- 2 teaspoons Dijon mustard
- 60g deli ham
- 60g Swiss, fontina, or Gruyère cheese
- ⅓ cup all-purpose flour
- 1 egg
- ½ cup breadcrumbs

Directions:

1. Pat the chicken breasts with a paper towel. Season the chicken with the salt. Pound the chicken breasts to 4cm thick. Create a pouch by slicing the side of each chicken breast. Spread 1 teaspoon Dijon mustard inside the pouch of each chicken breast. Wrap a 30g slice of ham around a 30g slice of cheese and place into the pouch. Repeat with the remaining ham and cheese.
2. In a medium bowl, place the flour.
3. In a second bowl, whisk the egg.
4. In a third bowl, place the breadcrumbs.
5. Dredge the chicken in the flour and shake off the excess. Next, dip the chicken into the egg and then in the breadcrumbs. Set the chicken on a plate and repeat with the remaining chicken piece.
6. Preheat the air fryer to 180°C/360°F.
7. Place the chicken in the air fryer basket and spray liberally with cooking spray. Cook for 8 minutes, turn the chicken breasts over, and liberally spray with cooking spray again; cook another 6 minutes. Once golden brown, check for an internal temperature of 75°C/165°F.

Variations & Ingredients Tips:

▶ Use different cheese like cheddar or provolone.
▶ Add spinach or sundried tomatoes to the filling.
▶ Substitute panko breadcrumbs for extra crunch.

Per Serving: Calories: 496; Total Fat: 17g; Saturated Fat: 7g; Cholesterol: 176mg; Sodium: 924mg; Total Carbs: 38g; Dietary Fiber: 1g; Total Sugars: 2g; Protein: 46g

Guajillo Chile Chicken Meatballs

Servings: 4 | Prep Time: 10 Minutes | Cooking Time: 30 Minutes

Ingredients:

- 450g ground chicken
- 1 large egg
- 1/2 cup bread crumbs
- 1 tbsp sour cream
- 2 tsp brown mustard
- 2 tbsp grated onion
- 2 tbsp tomato paste
- 1 tsp ground cumin
- 1 tsp guajillo chile powder
- 2 tbsp olive oil

Directions:

1. Preheat air fryer to 175°C/350°F.
2. Mix the ground chicken, egg, bread crumbs, sour cream, mustard, onion, tomato paste, cumin, and chili powder in a bowl. Form into 16 meatballs.
3. Place the meatballs in the greased frying basket and Air Fry for 8-10 minutes, shaking once until browned and cooked through.
4. Serve immediately.

Variations & Ingredients Tips:

▶ Use ground turkey for a leaner option.
▶ Add some minced garlic or cilantro to the mix.
▶ Serve with salsa, guacamole or queso fresco.

Per Serving: Calories: 330; Total Fat: 22g; Saturated Fat: 5g; Cholesterol: 165mg; Sodium: 270mg; Total Carbs: 7g; Dietary Fiber: 1g; Total Sugars: 2g; Protein: 27g

Mustardy Chicken Bites

Servings: 4 | Prep Time: 5 Minutes | Cooking Time: 20 Minutes + Chilling Time

Ingredients:

- 2 tbsp horseradish mustard
- 1 tbsp mayonnaise
- 1 tbsp olive oil
- 2 chicken breasts, cubed
- 1 tbsp parsley

Directions:

1. Combine all ingredients, excluding parsley, in a bowl. Let marinate covered in the fridge for 30 minutes.
2. Preheat air fryer at 175°C/350°F.
3. Place chicken cubes in the greased frying basket and Air Fry for 9 minutes, tossing once.
4. Serve immediately sprinkled with parsley.

Variations & Ingredients Tips:

- Use Dijon or whole grain mustard for a milder flavor.
- Add some honey or maple syrup to the marinade for sweetness.
- Serve skewered with cherry tomatoes and cucumber slices.

Per Serving: Calories: 150; Total Fat: 8g; Saturated Fat: 1g; Cholesterol: 75mg; Sodium: 220mg; Total Carbs: 1g; Dietary Fiber: 0g; Total Sugars: 0g; Protein: 19g

Easy Turkey Meatballs

Servings: 4 | Prep Time: 10 Minutes | Cooking Time: 20 Minutes

Ingredients:

- 450g ground turkey
- 1/2 celery stalk, chopped
- 1 egg
- 1/4 tsp red pepper flakes
- 1/4 cup bread crumbs
- Salt and pepper to taste
- 1/2 tsp garlic powder
- 1/2 tsp onion powder
- 1/2 tsp cayenne pepper

Directions:

1. Preheat air fryer to 180°C/360°F.
2. Add all of the ingredients to a bowl and mix well.
3. Shape the mixture into 12 balls and arrange them on the greased frying basket.
4. Air Fry for 10-12 minutes or until the meatballs are cooked through and browned.
5. Serve and enjoy!

Variations & Ingredients Tips:

- Add grated parmesan or pecorino romano cheese to the mix.
- Serve meatballs with your favorite marinara sauce or pesto.

- Use ground chicken instead of turkey for a milder flavor.

Per Serving: Calories: 240; Total Fat: 15g; Saturated Fat: 4g; Cholesterol: 130mg; Sodium: 180mg; Total Carbs: 4g; Dietary Fiber: 0g; Total Sugars: 1g; Protein: 24g

Berry-glazed Turkey Breast

Servings: 4 | Prep Time: 15 Minutes | Cooking Time: 1 Hour 25 Minutes

Ingredients:

- 1 bone-in, skin-on turkey breast
- 1 tbsp olive oil
- Salt and pepper to taste
- 1 cup raspberries
- 1 cup chopped strawberries
- 2 tbsp balsamic vinegar
- 2 tbsp butter, melted
- 1 tbsp honey mustard
- 1 tsp dried rosemary

Directions:

1. Preheat the air fryer to 180°C/350°F.
2. Lay the turkey breast skin-side up in the air fryer basket, brush with the oil, and sprinkle with salt and pepper.
3. Bake for 55-65 minutes, flipping twice.
4. Meanwhile, mix the berries, vinegar, melted butter, rosemary and honey mustard in a blender and blend until smooth.
5. Turn the turkey skin-side up inside the fryer and brush with half of the berry mix. Bake for 5 more minutes.
6. Put the remaining berry mix in a small saucepan and simmer for 3-4 minutes while the turkey cooks.
7. When the turkey is done, let it stand for 10 minutes, then carve. Serve with the remaining glaze.

Variations & Ingredients Tips:

- Use boneless, skinless turkey breast for quicker cooking time.
- Substitute raspberries and strawberries with blackberries, blueberries, or cranberries.
- Add a pinch of cayenne pepper or red pepper flakes to the glaze for a spicy kick.

Per Serving: Calories: 400; Total Fat: 15g; Saturated Fat: 5g; Sodium: 180mg; Total Carbohydrates: 14g; Dietary Fiber: 3g; Total Sugars: 10g; Protein: 52g

Irresistible Cheesy Chicken Sticks

Servings: 2 | Prep Time: 20 Minutes | Cooking Time: 30 Minutes

Ingredients:

- 6 mozzarella sticks
- 1 cup flour
- 2 eggs, beaten
- 450g ground chicken
- 1 1/2 cups breadcrumbs
- 1/4 tsp crushed chilis
- 1/4 tsp cayenne pepper
- 1/2 tsp garlic powder
- 1/4 tsp shallot powder
- 1/2 tsp oregano

Directions:

1. Preheat air fryer to 200°C/390°F.
2. Combine crushed chilis, cayenne pepper, garlic powder, shallot powder, and oregano in a bowl. Add the ground chicken and mix well with your hands until evenly combined.
3. In another mixing bowl, beat the eggs until fluffy and until the yolks and whites are fully combined, and set aside.
4. Pour the beaten eggs, flour, and bread crumbs into 3 separate bowls.
5. Roll the mozzarella sticks in the flour, then dip them in the beaten eggs. With hands, wrap the stick in a thin layer of the chicken mixture. Finally, coat the sticks in the crumbs.
6. Place the sticks in the greased frying basket fryer and Air Fry for 18-20 minutes, turning once until crispy.
7. Serve hot.

Variations & Ingredients Tips:

- Use pepper Jack cheese sticks for extra spice.
- Substitute ground chicken with Italian sausage or chorizo.
- Serve with marinara or ranch for dipping.

Per Serving: Calories: 860; Total Fat: 35g; Saturated Fat: 13g; Cholesterol: 360mg; Sodium: 1380mg; Total Carbs: 74g; Dietary Fiber: 4g; Total Sugars: 5g; Protein: 63g

Chicken Strips

Servings: 4 | Prep Time: 10 Minutes (plus 30 Minutes Marinating Time) | Cooking Time: 8 Minutes

Ingredients:

- 454 grams chicken tenders
- Marinade
- ¼ cup olive oil
- 2 tablespoons water
- 2 tablespoons honey
- 2 tablespoons white vinegar
- ½ teaspoon salt
- ½ teaspoon crushed red pepper
- 1 teaspoon garlic powder
- 1 teaspoon onion powder
- ½ teaspoon paprika

Directions:

1. Combine all marinade ingredients and mix well.
2. Add chicken and stir to coat. Cover tightly and let marinate in refrigerator for 30 minutes.
3. Remove tenders from marinade and place them in a single layer in the air fryer basket.
4. Cook at 200°C/390°F for 3 minutes. Turn tenders over and cook for 5 minutes longer or until chicken is done and juices run clear.
5. Repeat step 4 to cook remaining tenders.

Variations & Ingredients Tips:

- Use boneless, skinless chicken breasts cut into strips instead of tenders.
- Add a dash of Worcestershire sauce or soy sauce to the marinade for extra umami flavor.
- Serve with ranch dressing, honey mustard, or BBQ sauce for dipping.

Per Serving: Calories: 290; Total Fat: 15g; Saturated Fat: 2.5g; Sodium: 370mg; Total Carbohydrates: 9g; Dietary Fiber: 0g; Total Sugars: 8g; Protein: 30g

Kale & Rice Chicken Rolls

Servings: 4 | Prep Time: 15 Minutes | Cooking Time: 35 Minutes

Ingredients:

- 4 boneless, skinless chicken thighs
- 1/2 tsp ground fenugreek seeds

31

- 1 cup cooked wild rice
- 2 sundried tomatoes, diced
- 1/2 cup chopped kale
- 2 garlic cloves, minced
- 1 tsp salt
- 1 lemon, juiced
- 1/2 cup crumbled feta
- 1 tbsp olive oil

Directions:

1. Preheat air fryer to 190°C/380°F.
2. Put the chicken thighs between two pieces of plastic wrap, and using a meat mallet or a rolling pin, pound them out to about 6-mm thick.
3. Combine the rice, tomatoes, kale, garlic, salt, fenugreek seeds and lemon juice in a bowl and mix well.
4. Divide the rice mixture among the chicken thighs and sprinkle with feta. Fold the sides of the chicken thigh over the filling, and then gently place each of them seam-side down into the greased air frying basket. Drizzle the stuffed chicken thighs with olive oil.
5. Roast the stuffed chicken thighs for 12 minutes, then turn them over and cook for an additional 10 minutes.
6. Serve and enjoy!

Variations & Ingredients Tips:

- Use spinach or chard instead of kale.
- Add some chopped nuts like pistachios or pine nuts to the filling.
- Drizzle with tzatziki sauce before serving.

Per Serving: Calories: 370; Total Fat: 21g; Saturated Fat: 7g; Cholesterol: 145mg; Sodium: 900mg; Total Carbs: 17g; Dietary Fiber: 2g; Total Sugars: 2g; Protein: 32g

Nacho Chicken Fries

Servings: 4 | Prep Time: 15 Minutes | Cooking Time: 7 Minutes

Ingredients:

- 450g chicken tenders
- Salt
- 1/4 cup flour
- 2 eggs
- 3/4 cup panko breadcrumbs
- 3/4 cup crushed organic nacho cheese tortilla chips
- Oil for misting or cooking spray
- Seasoning Mix:
- 1 tablespoon chili powder
- 1 teaspoon ground cumin
- 1/2 teaspoon garlic powder
- 1/2 teaspoon onion powder

Directions:

1. Stir together all seasonings in a small cup and set aside.
2. Cut chicken tenders in half crosswise, then cut into strips no wider than about 1.25 cm.
3. Preheat air fryer to 200°C/390°F.
4. Salt chicken to taste. Place strips in large bowl and sprinkle with 1 tablespoon of the seasoning mix. Stir well to distribute seasonings.
5. Add flour to chicken and stir well to coat all sides.
6. Beat eggs together in a shallow dish.
7. In a second shallow dish, combine the panko, crushed chips, and the remaining 2 teaspoons of seasoning mix.
8. Dip chicken strips in eggs, then roll in crumbs. Mist with oil or cooking spray.
9. Chicken strips will cook best if done in two batches. They can be crowded and overlapping a little but not stacked in double or triple layers.
10. Cook for 4 minutes. Shake basket, mist with oil, and cook 3 more minutes, until chicken juices run clear and outside is crispy.
11. Repeat step 10 to cook remaining chicken fries.

Variations & Ingredients Tips:

- Use Cool Ranch Doritos or spicy nacho chips for different flavors.
- Dip chicken fries in queso, guacamole or salsa.
- Serve in tortillas with shredded lettuce, cheese and pico de gallo.

Per Serving: Calories: 360; Total Fat: 14g; Saturated Fat: 3g; Cholesterol: 175mg; Sodium: 620mg; Total Carbs: 25g; Dietary Fiber: 2g; Total Sugars: 1g; Protein: 33g

Rich Turkey Burgers

Servings: 4 | Prep Time: 10 Minutes | Cooking Time: 30 Minutes

Ingredients:

- 2 tbsp finely grated Emmental
- 1/3 cup minced onions
- ¼ cup grated carrots
- 2 garlic cloves, minced

- 2 tsp olive oil
- 1 tsp dried marjoram
- 1 egg
- 454 grams ground turkey

Directions:

1. Preheat air fryer to 200°C/400°F.
2. Mix the onions, carrots, garlic, olive oil, marjoram, Emmental, and egg in a bowl, then add the ground turkey. Use your hands to mix the ingredients together.
3. Form the mixture into 4 patties. Set them in the air fryer and Air Fry for 18-20 minutes, flipping once until cooked through and golden.
4. Serve.

Variations & Ingredients Tips:

- Use ground chicken, pork, or beef instead of turkey for different meats.
- Add chopped spinach, kale, or mushrooms to the patty mixture for extra veggies.
- Serve on a bun with lettuce, tomato, and your favorite condiments.

Per Serving: Calories: 290; Total Fat: 18g; Saturated Fat: 5g; Sodium: 170mg; Total Carbohydrates: 4g; Dietary Fiber: 1g; Total Sugars: 1g; Protein: 29g

Buttered Turkey Breasts

Servings: 6 | Prep Time: 15 Minutes | Cooking Time: 65 Minutes

Ingredients:

- ½ cup butter, melted
- 6 garlic cloves, minced
- 1 tsp dried oregano
- ½ tsp dried thyme
- ½ tsp dried rosemary
- Salt and pepper to taste
- 1.8 kg bone-in turkey breast
- 1 tbsp chopped cilantro

Directions:

1. Preheat air fryer to 180°C/350°F.
2. Combine butter, garlic, oregano, salt, and pepper in a small bowl.
3. Place the turkey breast on a plate and coat the entire turkey with the butter mixture.
4. Put the turkey breast-side down in the air fryer basket and scatter with thyme and rosemary. Bake for 20 minutes.
5. Flip the turkey so that the breast side is up, then bake for another 20-30 minutes until it has an internal temperature of 74°C/165°F.
6. Allow to rest for 10 minutes before carving. Serve sprinkled with cilantro.

Variations & Ingredients Tips:

- Use boneless, skinless turkey breast for quicker cooking time.
- Add a pinch of paprika or red pepper flakes to the butter mixture for a smoky or spicy flavor.
- Serve with cranberry sauce, gravy, or a side of roasted vegetables.

Per Serving: Calories: 580; Total Fat: 32g; Saturated Fat: 15g; Sodium: 330mg; Total Carbohydrates: 2g; Dietary Fiber: 0g; Total Sugars: 0g; Protein: 71g

Nashville Hot Chicken

Servings: 4 | Prep Time: 20 Minutes | Cooking Time: 27 Minutes

Ingredients:

- 1 (1.8kg) chicken, cut into 6 pieces (2 breasts, 2 thighs and 2 drumsticks)
- 2 eggs
- 1 cup buttermilk
- 2 cups all-purpose flour
- 2 tablespoons paprika
- 1 teaspoon garlic powder
- 1 teaspoon onion powder
- 2 teaspoons salt
- 1 teaspoon freshly ground black pepper
- Vegetable oil, in a spray bottle
- Nashville Hot Sauce:
- 1 tablespoon cayenne pepper
- 1 teaspoon salt
- 1/4 cup vegetable oil
- 4 slices white bread
- Dill pickle slices

Directions:

1. Cut the chicken breasts into 2 pieces so that you have a total of 8 pieces of chicken.
2. Set up a two-stage dredging station. Whisk the eggs and buttermilk together in a bowl. Combine the flour, paprika, garlic powder, onion powder, salt and black pepper in a zipper-sealable plastic bag. Dip the chicken pieces into the egg-buttermilk mixture, then toss them in the seasoned flour, coating all sides. Repeat this pro-

cedure (egg mixture and then flour mixture) one more time. This can be a little messy, but make sure all sides of the chicken are completely covered. Spray the chicken with vegetable oil and set aside.
3. Preheat the air fryer to 190°C/370°F. Spray or brush the bottom of the air-fryer basket with a little vegetable oil.
4. Air-fry the chicken in two batches at 190°C/370°F for 20 minutes, flipping the pieces over halfway through the cooking process. Transfer the chicken to a plate, but do not cover. Repeat with the second batch of chicken.
5. Lower the temperature on the air fryer to 170°C/340°F. Flip the chicken back over and place the first batch of chicken on top of the second batch already in the basket. Air-fry for another 7 minutes.
6. While the chicken is air-frying, combine the cayenne pepper and salt in a bowl. Heat the vegetable oil in a small saucepan and when it is very hot, add it to the spice mix, whisking until smooth. It will sizzle briefly when you add it to the spices.
7. Place the fried chicken on top of the white bread slices and brush the hot sauce all over chicken. Top with the pickle slices and serve warm. Enjoy the heat and the flavor!

Variations & Ingredients Tips:

- ▶ Adjust the cayenne to your spice preference.
- ▶ Use chicken tenders for easier prep and cooking.
- ▶ Serve in a sandwich with coleslaw and comeback sauce.

Per Serving: Calories: 860; Total Fat: 58g; Saturated Fat: 12g; Cholesterol: 290mg; Sodium: 2210mg; Total Carbs: 36g; Dietary Fiber: 2g; Total Sugars: 5g; Protein: 55g

Simple Salsa Chicken Thighs

Servings: 2 | Prep Time: 5 Minutes | Cooking Time: 35 Minutes

Ingredients:

- 454 grams boneless, skinless chicken thighs
- 1 cup mild chunky salsa
- ½ tsp taco seasoning
- 2 lime wedges for serving

Directions:

1. Preheat air fryer to 180°C/350°F.
2. Add chicken thighs into a baking pan and pour salsa and taco seasoning over.
3. Place the pan in the air fryer basket and Air Fry for 30 minutes until golden brown.
4. Serve with lime wedges.

Variations & Ingredients Tips:

- ▶ Use spicy salsa or add diced jalapeños for a kick of heat.
- ▶ Sprinkle with shredded cheddar cheese during the last 5 minutes of cooking.
- ▶ Serve over rice, quinoa, or in tortillas for tacos.

Per Serving: Calories: 330; Total Fat: 11g; Saturated Fat: 3g; Sodium: 950mg; Total Carbohydrates: 10g; Dietary Fiber: 2g; Total Sugars: 6g; Protein: 45g

Hawaiian Chicken

Servings: 4 | Prep Time: 10 Minutes | Cooking Time: 25 Minutes

Ingredients:

- 1 can (400g) diced pineapple
- 1 kiwi, sliced
- 2 tbsp coconut aminos
- 1 tbsp honey
- 3 garlic cloves, minced
- Salt and pepper to taste
- 1/2 tsp paprika
- 450g chicken breasts

Directions:

1. Preheat air fryer to 180°C/360°F.
2. Stir together pineapple, kiwi, coconut aminos, honey, garlic, salt, paprika, and pepper in a small bowl.
3. Arrange the chicken in a single layer in a baking dish. Spread half of the pineapple mixture over the top of the chicken. Transfer the dish into the frying basket.
4. Roast for 8 minutes, then flip the chicken. Spread the rest of the pineapple mixture over the top of the chicken and Roast for another 8-10 until the chicken is done.
5. Allow sitting for 5 minutes. Serve and enjoy!

Variations & Ingredients Tips:

- ▶ Use boneless, skinless chicken thighs for juicier meat.
- ▶ Add some red pepper flakes for a spicy kick.
- ▶ Garnish with chopped macadamia nuts and green onions.

Per Serving: Calories: 270; Total Fat: 4g; Saturated Fat:

1g; Cholesterol: 85mg; Sodium: 310mg; Total Carbs: 25g; Dietary Fiber: 2g; Total Sugars: 20g; Protein: 32g

Party Buffalo Chicken Drumettes

Servings: 6 | Prep Time: 5 Minutes | Cooking Time: 30 Minutes

Ingredients:

- 16 chicken drumettes
- 1 tsp garlic powder
- 1 tbsp chicken seasoning
- Black pepper to taste
- 1/4 cup Buffalo wings sauce
- 2 spring onions, sliced

Directions:

1. Preheat air fryer to 200°C/400°F.
2. Sprinkle garlic, chicken seasoning, and black pepper on the drumettes. Place them in the fryer and spray with cooking oil.
3. Air Fry for 10 minutes, shaking the basket once. Transfer the drumettes to a large bowl.
4. Drizzle with Buffalo wing sauce and toss to coat. Place in the fryer and Fry for 7-8 minutes, until crispy.
5. Allow to cool slightly. Top with spring onions and serve warm.

Variations & Ingredients Tips:

- Use honey BBQ or teriyaki sauce instead of Buffalo for different flavors.
- Add a pinch of cayenne or red pepper flakes for extra heat.
- Serve with celery sticks and blue cheese dressing.

Per Serving: Calories: 200; Total Fat: 12g; Saturated Fat: 3.5g; Cholesterol: 70mg; Sodium: 530mg; Total Carbs: 2g; Dietary Fiber: 0g; Total Sugars: 0g; Protein: 19g

Spinach And Feta Stuffed Chicken Breasts

Servings: 4 | Prep Time: 15 Minutes | Cooking Time: 27 Minutes

Ingredients:

- 1 (285g) package frozen spinach, thawed and drained well
- 1 cup feta cheese, crumbled
- 1/2 teaspoon freshly ground black pepper
- 4 boneless chicken breasts
- Salt and freshly ground black pepper
- 1 tablespoon olive oil

Directions:

1. Prepare the filling. Squeeze out as much liquid as possible from the thawed spinach. Rough chop the spinach and transfer it to a mixing bowl with the feta cheese and the freshly ground black pepper.
2. Prepare the chicken breast. Place the chicken breast on a cutting board and press down on the chicken breast with one hand to keep it stabilized. Make an incision about 2.5cm long in the fattest side of the breast. Move the knife up and down inside the chicken breast, without poking through either the top or the bottom, or the other side of the breast. The inside pocket should be about 7.5cm long, but the opening should only be about 2.5cm wide. If this is too difficult, you can make the incision longer, but you will have to be more careful when cooking the chicken breast since this will expose more of the stuffing.
3. Once you have prepared the chicken breasts, use your fingers to stuff the filling into each pocket, spreading the mixture down as far as you can.
4. Preheat the air fryer to 195°C/380°F.
5. Lightly brush or spray the air fryer basket and the chicken breasts with olive oil. Transfer two of the stuffed chicken breasts to the air fryer. Air-fry for 12 minutes, turning the chicken breasts over halfway through the cooking time. Remove the chicken to a resting plate and air-fry the second two breasts for 12 minutes. Return the first batch of chicken to the air fryer with the second batch and air-fry for 3 more minutes. When the chicken is cooked, an instant read thermometer should register 75°C/165°F in the thickest part of the chicken, as well as in the stuffing.
6. Remove the chicken breasts and let them rest on a cutting board for 2 to 3 minutes. Slice the chicken on the bias and serve with the slices fanned out.

Variations & Ingredients Tips:

- Use fresh spinach instead of frozen.
- Substitute feta for goat cheese or shredded mozzarella.
- Add sun-dried tomatoes or pine nuts to the stuffing mixture.

Per Serving: Calories: 332; Total Fat: 14g; Saturated Fat: 7g; Cholesterol: 143mg; Sodium: 599mg; Total

Carbs: 6g; Dietary Fiber: 2g; Total Sugars: 2g; Protein: 44g

Peachy Chicken Chunks With Cherries

Servings: 4 | Prep Time: 10 Minutes | Cooking Time: 16 Minutes

Ingredients:

- 1/3 cup peach preserves
- 1 teaspoon ground rosemary
- 1/2 teaspoon black pepper
- 1/2 teaspoon salt
- 1/2 teaspoon marjoram
- 1 teaspoon light olive oil
- 450g boneless chicken breasts, cut in 4-cm chunks
- Oil for misting or cooking spray
- 280g package frozen unsweetened dark cherries, thawed and drained

Directions:

1. In a medium bowl, mix together peach preserves, rosemary, pepper, salt, marjoram, and olive oil.
2. Stir in chicken chunks and toss to coat well with the preserve mixture.
3. Spray air fryer basket with oil or cooking spray and lay chicken chunks in basket.
4. Cook at 200°C/390°F for 7 minutes. Stir. Cook for 8 more minutes or until chicken juices run clear.
5. When chicken has cooked through, scatter the cherries over and cook for additional minute to heat cherries.

Variations & Ingredients Tips:

- Use apricot or mango preserves for a different fruity flavor.
- Add some chopped jalapenos or red pepper flakes for a spicy-sweet combo.
- Serve over rice or quinoa with steamed broccoli on the side.

Per Serving: Calories: 290; Total Fat: 6g; Saturated Fat: 1.5g; Cholesterol: 100mg; Sodium: 370mg; Total Carbs: 25g; Dietary Fiber: 1g; Total Sugars: 21g; Protein: 35g

Spicy Black Bean Turkey Burgers With Cumin-avocado Spread

Servings: 2 | Prep Time: 10 Minutes | Cooking Time: 20 Minutes

Ingredients:

- 1 cup canned black beans, drained and rinsed
- 340g lean ground turkey
- 2 tablespoons minced red onion
- 1 Jalapeño pepper, seeded and minced
- 2 tablespoons plain breadcrumbs
- 1/2 teaspoon chili powder
- 1/4 teaspoon cayenne pepper
- Salt, to taste
- Olive or vegetable oil
- 2 slices pepper jack cheese
- Toasted burger rolls, sliced tomatoes, lettuce leaves
- Cumin-Avocado Spread:
- 1 ripe avocado
- Juice of 1 lime
- 1 teaspoon ground cumin
- 1/2 teaspoon salt
- 1 tablespoon chopped fresh cilantro
- Freshly ground black pepper

Directions:

1. Place the black beans in a large bowl and smash them slightly with the back of a fork. Add the ground turkey, red onion, Jalapeño pepper, breadcrumbs, chili powder and cayenne pepper. Season with salt. Mix with your hands to combine all the ingredients and then shape them into 2 patties. Brush both sides of the burger patties with a little olive or vegetable oil.
2. Preheat the air fryer to 190°C/380°F.
3. Transfer the burgers to the air fryer basket and air-fry for 20 minutes, flipping them over halfway through the cooking process. Top the burgers with the pepper jack cheese (securing the slices to the burgers with a toothpick) for the last 2 minutes of the cooking process.
4. While the burgers are cooking, make the cumin avocado spread. Place the avocado, lime juice, cumin and salt in food processor and process until smooth. (For a chunkier spread, you can mash this by hand in a bowl.) Stir in the cilantro and season with freshly ground black pepper. Chill the spread until you are ready to serve.

5. When the burgers have finished cooking, remove them from the air fryer and let them rest on a plate, covered gently with aluminum foil. Brush a little olive oil on the insides of the burger rolls. Place the rolls, cut side up, into the air fryer basket and air-fry at 200°C/400°F for 1 minute to toast and warm them.
6. Spread the cumin-avocado spread on the rolls and build your burgers with lettuce and sliced tomatoes and any other ingredient you like. Serve warm with a side of sweet potato fries.

Variations & Ingredients Tips:

- Use black bean veggie patties instead of turkey for a vegetarian option.
- Add crumbled feta or shredded cheddar to the burger patty mixture.
- Serve on whole wheat buns or lettuce wraps.

Per Serving (1 burger + spread): Calories: 566; Total Fat: 24g; Saturated Fat: 6g; Cholesterol: 115mg; Sodium: 647mg; Total Carbs: 46g; Dietary Fiber: 14g; Total Sugars: 4g; Protein: 43g

Chicken Flautas

Servings: 6 | Prep Time: 15 Minutes | Cooking Time: 8 Minutes

Ingredients:

- 6 tablespoons whipped cream cheese
- 1 cup shredded cooked chicken
- 6 tablespoons mild pico de gallo salsa
- 1/3 cup shredded Mexican cheese
- 1/2 teaspoon taco seasoning
- Six 20-cm flour tortillas
- 2 cups shredded lettuce
- 1/2 cup guacamole

Directions:

1. Preheat the air fryer to 190°C/370°F.
2. In a bowl, mix the cream cheese, chicken, salsa, shredded cheese, and taco seasoning.
3. Lay the tortillas out and divide the chicken mixture evenly among them, leaving 2.5-cm from edges.
4. Spray basket with oil. Roll up flautas and place seam-side down in basket. Mist tops with oil.
5. Cook in batches if needed, for 7 minutes until browned.
6. Serve warm over shredded lettuce with guacamole on top.

Variations & Ingredients Tips:

- Use corn tortillas instead of flour for a crispier texture.
- Add refried beans or Mexican rice as a side.
- Top with crumbled queso fresco or pico de gallo.

Per Serving (2 flautas): Calories: 313; Total Fat: 17g; Saturated Fat: 6g; Cholesterol: 54mg; Sodium: 652mg; Total Carbs: 26g; Dietary Fiber: 3g; Total Sugars: 2g; Protein: 15g

Beef, Pork & Lamb Recipes

Lamb Meatballs With Quick Tomato Sauce

Servings: 4 | Prep Time: 20 Minutes | Cooking Time: 8 Minutes

Ingredients:

- ½ small onion, finely diced
- 1 clove garlic, minced
- 450 g ground lamb
- 2 tablespoons fresh parsley, finely chopped (plus more for garnish)
- 2 teaspoons fresh oregano, finely chopped
- 2 tablespoons milk
- 1 egg yolk
- Salt and freshly ground black pepper
- ½ cup crumbled feta cheese, for garnish

- Tomato Sauce:
- 2 tablespoons butter
- 1 clove garlic, smashed
- Pinch crushed red pepper flakes
- ¼ teaspoon ground cinnamon
- 1 (800 g) can crushed tomatoes
- Salt, to taste

Directions:

1. Combine all ingredients for the meatballs in a large bowl and mix just until everything is combined. Shape the mixture into 4 cm balls or shape the meat between two spoons to make quenelles (little three-sided footballs).
2. Preheat the air fryer to 200°C/400°F.
3. While the air fryer is preheating, start the quick tomato sauce. Place the butter, garlic and red pepper flakes in a sauté pan and heat over medium heat on the stovetop. Let the garlic sizzle a little, but before the butter starts to brown, add the cinnamon and tomatoes. Bring to a simmer and simmer for 15 minutes. Season to taste with salt (but not too much as the feta that you will be sprinkling on at the end will be salty).
4. Brush the bottom of the air fryer basket with a little oil and transfer the meatballs to the air fryer basket in one layer, air-frying in batches if necessary.
5. Air-fry at 200°C/400°F for 8 minutes, giving the basket a shake once during the cooking process to turn the meatballs over.
6. To serve, spoon a pool of the tomato sauce onto plates and add the meatballs in a decorative manner. Sprinkle the feta cheese on top and garnish with more fresh parsley. Serve immediately.

Variations & Ingredients Tips:

- Use different types of cheese, such as goat cheese or Parmesan, for a variety of flavors.
- Add some chopped Kalamata olives or capers to the tomato sauce for a briny flavor.
- Serve the meatballs with a side of pasta or crusty bread for a complete meal.

Per Serving: Calories: 510; Total Fat: 38g; Saturated Fat: 18g; Cholesterol: 170mg; Sodium: 780mg; Total Carbs: 15g; Fiber: 3g; Sugars: 8g; Protein: 31g

Perfect Pork Chops

Servings: 3 | Prep Time: 5 Minutes | Cooking Time: 10 Minutes

Ingredients:

- ¾ teaspoon mild paprika
- ¾ teaspoon dried thyme
- ¾ teaspoon onion powder
- ¼ teaspoon garlic powder
- ¼ teaspoon table salt
- ¼ teaspoon ground black pepper
- 3 boneless center-cut pork loin chops (170 g each)
- Vegetable oil spray

Directions:

1. Preheat the air fryer to 200°C/400°F.
2. Mix the paprika, thyme, onion powder, garlic powder, salt, and pepper in a small bowl until well combined. Massage this mixture into both sides of the chops. Generously coat both sides of the chops with vegetable oil spray.
3. When the machine is at temperature, set the chops in the basket with as much air space between them as possible. Air-fry undisturbed for 10 minutes, or until an instant-read meat thermometer inserted into the thickest part of a chop registers 65°C/145°F.
4. Use kitchen tongs to transfer the chops to a cutting board or serving plates. Cool for 5 minutes before serving.

Variations & Ingredients Tips:

- Use different types of seasoning, such as Cajun or Italian, for a variety of flavors.
- Add some minced garlic or red pepper flakes to the seasoning mixture for extra flavor.
- Serve the pork chops with a side of roasted vegetables or mashed potatoes for a complete meal.

Per Serving: Calories: 260; Total Fat: 13g; Saturated Fat: 4g; Cholesterol: 105mg; Sodium: 300mg; Total Carbs: 1g; Fiber: 0g; Sugars: 0g; Protein: 35g

Chipotle Pork Meatballs

Servings: 4 | Prep Time: 15 Minutes | Cooking Time: 35 Minutes

Ingredients:

- 450 g ground pork
- 1 egg
- ¼ cup chipotle sauce
- ¼ cup grated celery
- ¼ cup chopped parsley

- ¼ cup chopped cilantro
- ¼ cup flour
- ¼ teaspoon salt

Directions:

1. Preheat air fryer to 180°C/350°F. In a large bowl, combine the ground pork, egg, chipotle sauce, celery, parsley, cilantro, flour, and salt. Form mixture into 16 meatballs.
2. Place the meatballs in the lightly greased frying basket and Air Fry for 8-10 minutes, flipping once.
3. Serve immediately!

Variations & Ingredients Tips:

- Use different types of meat, such as beef or turkey, for a variety of flavors and textures.
- Add some minced garlic or onion to the meatball mixture for extra flavor.
- Serve the meatballs with a side of rice or beans for a complete meal.

Per Serving: Calories: 340; Total Fat: 22g; Saturated Fat: 8g; Cholesterol: 135mg; Sodium: 570mg; Total Carbs: 9g; Fiber: 1g; Sugars: 1g; Protein: 26g

Delicious Juicy Pork Meatballs

Servings: 4 | Prep Time: 10 Minutes | Cooking Time: 35 Minutes

Ingredients:

- ¼ cup grated cheddar cheese
- 450 g ground pork
- 1 egg
- 1 tablespoon Greek yogurt
- ½ teaspoon onion powder
- ¼ cup chopped parsley
- 2 tablespoons bread crumbs
- ¼ teaspoon garlic powder
- Salt and pepper to taste

Directions:

1. Preheat air fryer to 180°C/350°F.
2. In a bowl, combine the ground pork, egg, yogurt, onion, parsley, cheddar cheese, bread crumbs, garlic, salt, and black pepper. Form mixture into 16 meatballs.
3. Place meatballs in the lightly greased frying basket and Air Fry for 8-10 minutes, flipping once.
4. Serve.

Variations & Ingredients Tips:

- Use different types of cheese, such as mozzarella or Parmesan, for a variety of flavors.
- Add some minced jalapeño or red pepper flakes to the meatball mixture for a spicy kick.
- Serve the meatballs with a side of tomato sauce or barbecue sauce for dipping.

Per Serving: Calories: 320; Total Fat: 22g; Saturated Fat: 9g; Cholesterol: 135mg; Sodium: 280mg; Total Carbs: 5g; Fiber: 0g; Sugars: 1g; Protein: 27g

Italian Sausage & Peppers

Servings: 6 | Prep Time: 20 Minutes | Cooking Time: 25 Minutes

Ingredients:

- 1 170g can tomato paste
- 2/3 cup water
- 1 225g can tomato sauce
- 1 teaspoon dried parsley flakes
- 1/2 teaspoon garlic powder
- 1/8 teaspoon oregano
- 225g mild Italian bulk sausage
- 1 tablespoon extra virgin olive oil
- 1/2 large onion, cut in 2.5cm chunks
- 113g fresh mushrooms, sliced
- 1 large green bell pepper, cut in 2.5cm chunks
- 227g spaghetti, cooked
- Parmesan cheese for serving

Directions:

1. In a large saucepan or skillet, stir together the tomato paste, water, tomato sauce, parsley, garlic, and oregano. Heat on stovetop over very low heat while preparing meat and vegetables.
2. Break sausage into small chunks, about 1.25cm pieces. Place in air fryer baking pan.
3. Cook at 390°F/199°C for 5 minutes. Stir. Cook 7 minutes longer or until sausage is well done. Remove from pan, drain on paper towels, and add to the sauce mixture.
4. If any sausage grease remains in baking pan, pour it off or use paper towels to soak it up. (Be careful handling that hot pan!)
5. Place olive oil, onions, and mushrooms in pan and stir. Cook for 5 minutes or just until tender. Using a slotted spoon, transfer onions and mushrooms from baking pan into the sauce and sausage mixture.

6. Place bell pepper chunks in air fryer baking pan and cook for 8 minutes or until tender. When done, stir into sauce with sausage and other vegetables.
7. Serve over cooked spaghetti with plenty of Parmesan cheese.

Variations & Ingredients Tips:

- Use hot or sweet Italian sausage for more or less spice
- Add sliced zucchini, eggplant or other veggies to the mix
- Finish with a splash of red wine or balsamic vinegar for extra flavor

Per Serving: Calories: 316; Total Fat: 16g; Saturated Fat: 5g; Cholesterol: 41mg; Sodium: 920mg; Total Carbs: 27g; Dietary Fiber: 4g; Total Sugars: 9g; Protein: 17g

Kielbasa Chunks With Pineapple & Peppers

Servings: 2 | Prep Time: 5 Minutes | Cooking Time: 10 Minutes

Ingredients:

- 340g kielbasa sausage
- 240g bell pepper chunks (any color)
- 227g can pineapple chunks in juice, drained
- 1 tablespoon barbeque seasoning
- 1 tablespoon soy sauce
- Cooking spray

Directions:

1. Cut sausage into 25cm slices.
2. In a medium bowl, toss all ingredients together.
3. Spray air fryer basket with nonstick cooking spray.
4. Pour sausage mixture into the basket.
5. Cook at 390°F/199°C for approximately 5 minutes. Shake basket and cook an additional 5 minutes.

Variations & Ingredients Tips:

- Use turkey or chicken sausage for a leaner option
- Add thinly sliced onions or shallots to the mix
- Drizzle with teriyaki sauce instead of soy sauce

Per Serving: Calories: 505; Total Fat: 36g; Saturated Fat: 12g; Cholesterol: 105mg; Sodium: 2090mg; Total Carbs: 36g; Dietary Fiber: 3g; Total Sugars: 21g; Protein: 17g

Indonesian Pork Satay

Servings: 4 | Prep Time: 20 Minutes | Cooking Time: 30 Minutes

Ingredients:

- 450g pork tenderloin, cubed
- 1/4 cup minced onion
- 2 garlic cloves, minced
- 1 jalapeño pepper, minced
- 2 tbsp lime juice
- 2 tbsp coconut milk
- 1/2 tbsp ground coriander
- 1/2 tsp ground cumin
- 2 tbsp peanut butter
- 2 tsp curry powder

Directions:

1. Combine the pork, onion, garlic, jalapeño, lime juice, coconut milk, peanut butter, ground coriander, cumin, and curry powder in a bowl. Stir well and allow to marinate for 10 minutes.
2. Preheat air fryer to 380°F/193°C. Use a holey spoon and take the pork out of the marinade and set the marinade aside. Poke 8 bamboo skewers through the meat, then place the skewers in the air fryer. Use a cooking brush to rub the marinade on each skewer, then Grill for 10-14 minutes, adding more marinade if necessary. The pork should be golden and cooked through when finished. Serve warm.

Variations & Ingredients Tips:

- Use chicken instead of pork for chicken satay
- Add some brown sugar or honey to the marinade for a sweet and savory flavor
- Serve with peanut dipping sauce and cucumber salad on the side

Per Serving: Calories: 325; Total Fat: 14g; Saturated Fat: 4g; Cholesterol: 95mg; Sodium: 220mg; Total Carbs: 11g; Dietary Fiber: 2g; Total Sugars: 3g; Protein: 36g

Easy Tex-mex Chimichangas

Servings: 2 | Prep Time: 10 Minutes | Cooking Time: 8 Minutes

Ingredients:

- 115 g thinly sliced deli roast beef, chopped
- ½ cup (about 55 g) shredded Cheddar cheese

or shredded Tex-Mex cheese blend
- ¼ cup jarred salsa verde or salsa rojo
- ½ teaspoon ground cumin
- ½ teaspoon dried oregano
- 2 burrito-size (30 cm) flour tortilla(s), not corn tortillas (gluten-free, if a concern)
- ⅔ cup canned refried beans
- Vegetable oil spray

Directions:

1. Preheat the air fryer to 190°C/375°F.
2. Stir the roast beef, cheese, salsa, cumin, and oregano in a bowl until well mixed.
3. Lay a tortilla on a clean, dry work surface. Spread ⅓ cup of the refried beans in the center lower third of the tortilla(s), leaving an 2.5-cm on either side of the spread beans.
4. For one chimichanga, spread all of the roast beef mixture on top of the beans. For two, spread half of the roast beef mixture on each tortilla.
5. At either "end" of the filling mixture, fold the sides of the tortilla up and over the filling, partially covering it. Starting with the unfolded side of the tortilla just below the filling, roll the tortilla closed. Fold and roll the second filled tortilla, as necessary.
6. Coat the exterior of the tortilla(s) with vegetable oil spray. Set the chimichanga(s) seam side down in the basket, with at least 1.25 cm air space between them if you're working with two. Air-fry undisturbed for 8 minutes, or until the tortilla is lightly browned and crisp.
7. Use kitchen tongs to gently transfer the chimichanga(s) to a wire rack. Cool for at last 5 minutes or up to 20 minutes before serving.

Variations & Ingredients Tips:

- Use different types of meat, such as chicken or pork, for a variety of flavors and textures.
- Add some diced onion or bell pepper to the filling for extra vegetables.
- Serve the chimichangas with sour cream, guacamole, or extra salsa for dipping.

Per Serving: Calories: 520; Total Fat: 25g; Saturated Fat: 11g; Cholesterol: 65mg; Sodium: 1400mg; Total Carbs: 45g; Fiber: 6g; Sugars: 3g; Protein: 30g

Traditional Italian Beef Meatballs

Servings: 4 | Prep Time: 15 Minutes | Cooking Time: 35 Minutes

Ingredients:

- 1/3 cup grated Parmesan
- 450-g ground beef
- 1 egg, beaten
- 2 tbsp tomato paste
- 1/2 tsp Italian seasonings
- 1/4 cup ricotta cheese
- 3 cloves garlic, minced
- 1/4 cup grated yellow onion
- Salt and pepper to taste
- 1/4 cup almond flour
- 1/4 cup chopped basil
- 2 cups marinara sauce

Directions:

1. Preheat air fryer to 400°F/205°C. In a large bowl, combine ground beef, egg, tomato paste, Italian seasoning, ricotta cheese, Parmesan cheese, garlic, onion, salt, pepper, flour, and basil. Form mixture into 4 meatballs. Add them to the greased frying basket and Air Fry for 20 minutes. Warm the marinara sauce in a skillet over medium heat for 3 minutes. Add in cooked meatballs and roll them around in sauce for 2 minutes. Serve with sauce over the top.

Variations & Ingredients Tips:

- Use a mix of ground beef, pork and veal for more authentic flavor
- Substitute breadcrumbs for the almond flour
- Add grated pecorino romano or asiago cheese

Per Serving: Calories: 440; Total Fat: 24g; Saturated Fat: 10g; Cholesterol: 145mg; Sodium: 920mg; Total Carbs: 23g; Dietary Fiber: 3g; Total Sugars: 8g; Protein: 32g

Crispy Five-spice Pork Belly

Servings: 6 | Prep Time: 20 Minutes | Cooking Time: 60-75 Minutes

Ingredients:

- 680 g pork belly with skin
- 3 tablespoons Shaoxing (Chinese cooking rice wine), dry sherry, or white grape juice
- 1½ teaspoons granulated white sugar
- ¾ teaspoon five-spice powder
- 1¼ cups coarse sea salt or kosher salt

Directions:

1. Preheat the air fryer to 180°C/350°F.
2. Set the pork belly skin side up on a cutting board. Use a meat fork to make dozens and dozens of tiny holes all across the surface of the skin. You can hardly make too many holes. These will allow the skin to bubble up and keep it from becoming hard as it roasts.
3. Turn the pork belly over so that one of its longer sides faces you. Make four evenly spaced vertical slits in the meat. The slits should go about halfway into the meat toward the fat.
4. Mix the Shaoxing or its substitute, sugar, and five-spice powder in a small bowl until the sugar dissolves. Massage this mixture across the meat and into the cuts.
5. Turn the pork belly over again. Blot dry any moisture on the skin. Make a double-thickness aluminum foil tray by setting two 25 cm long pieces of foil on top of another. Set the pork belly skin side up in the center of this tray. Fold the sides of the tray up toward the pork, crimping the foil as you work to make a high-sided case all around the pork belly. Seal the foil to the meat on all sides so that only the skin is exposed.
6. Pour the salt onto the skin and pat it down and in place to create a crust. Pick up the foil tray with the pork in it and set it in the basket.
7. Air-fry undisturbed for 35 minutes for a small batch, 45 minutes for a medium batch, or 50 minutes for a large batch.
8. Remove the foil tray with the pork belly still in it. Warning: The foil tray is full of scalding-hot fat. Discard the fat in the tray (not down the drain!), as well as the tray itself. Transfer the pork belly to a cutting board.
9. Raise the air fryer temperature to 190°C/375°F (or 200°C/380°F or 200°C/390°F, if one of these is the closest setting). Brush the salt crust off the pork, removing any visible salt from the sides of the meat, too.
10. When the machine is at temperature, return the pork belly skin side up to the basket. Air-fry undisturbed for 25 minutes, or until crisp and very well browned. If the machine is at 200°C/390°F, you may be able to shave 5 minutes off the cooking time so that the skin doesn't blacken.
11. Use a nonstick-safe spatula, and perhaps a silicone baking mitt, to transfer the pork belly to a wire rack. Cool for 10 minutes before serving.

Variations & Ingredients Tips:

- Use different types of sugar, such as brown sugar or honey, for a variety of flavors.
- Add some minced garlic or ginger to the five-spice mixture for extra flavor.
- Serve the pork belly with a side of steamed rice or stir-fried vegetables for a complete meal.

Per Serving: Calories: 540; Total Fat: 47g; Saturated Fat: 17g; Cholesterol: 85mg; Sodium: 11660mg; Total Carbs: 6g; Fiber: 0g; Sugars: 3g; Protein: 18g

Peppered Steak Bites

Servings: 4 | Prep Time: 10 Minutes | Cooking Time: 14 Minutes

Ingredients:

- 450 g sirloin steak, cut into 2.5 cm cubes
- ½ teaspoon coarse sea salt
- 1 teaspoon coarse black pepper
- 2 teaspoons Worcestershire sauce
- ½ teaspoon garlic powder
- ¼ teaspoon red pepper flakes
- ¼ cup chopped parsley

Directions:

1. Preheat the air fryer to 200°C/390°F.
2. In a large bowl, place the steak cubes and toss with the salt, pepper, Worcestershire sauce, garlic powder, and red pepper flakes.
3. Pour the steak into the air fryer basket and cook for 10 to 14 minutes, depending on how well done you prefer your bites. Starting at the 8-minute mark, toss the steak bites every 2 minutes to check for doneness.
4. When the steak is cooked, remove it from the basket to a serving bowl and top with the chopped parsley. Allow the steak to rest for 5 minutes before serving.

Variations & Ingredients Tips:

- Use different cuts of steak, such as ribeye or tenderloin, for a variety of flavors and textures.
- Add some sliced onions or bell peppers to the steak for extra vegetables.
- Serve the steak bites with a side of roasted potatoes or a salad for a complete meal.

Per Serving: Calories: 220; Total Fat: 11g; Saturated Fat: 4g; Cholesterol: 85mg; Sodium: 420mg; Total Carbs: 1g; Fiber: 0g; Sugars: 0g; Protein: 29g

Argentinian Steak Asado Salad

Servings: 2 | Prep Time: 15 Minutes | Cooking

Time: 35 Minutes

Ingredients:

- 1 jalapeño pepper, sliced thin
- ¼ cup shredded pepper Jack cheese
- 1 avocado, peeled and pitted
- ¼ cup diced tomatoes
- ½ diced shallot
- 2 teaspoons chopped cilantro
- 2 teaspoons lime juice
- 400g flank steak
- 1 garlic clove, minced
- 1 teaspoon ground cumin
- Salt and pepper to taste
- ¼ lime
- 3 cups mesclun mix
- ½ cup pico de gallo

Directions:

1. Mash the avocado in a small bowl. Add tomatoes, shallot, cilantro, lime juice, salt, and pepper. Set aside.
2. Season the steak with garlic, salt, pepper, and cumin.
3. Preheat air fryer to 200°C/400°F. Put the steak into the greased frying basket. Bake 8-10 minutes, flipping once until your desired doneness. Remove and let rest. Squeeze the lime over the steak and cut into thin slices.
4. For one serving, plate half of mesclun, 2 tablespoons of cheese, and ¼ cup guacamole. Place half of the steak slices on top, then add ¼ cup pico de gallo and jalapeño if desired.

Variations & Ingredients Tips:

- Use different types of greens, such as romaine or spinach, for a variety of flavors and textures.
- Add some cooked black beans or corn for extra fiber and nutrients.
- For a spicier version, add some chipotle pepper or hot sauce to the guacamole or pico de gallo.

Per Serving: Calories: 460; Total Fat: 29g; Saturated Fat: 8g; Cholesterol: 100mg; Sodium: 630mg; Total Carbs: 17g; Fiber: 8g; Sugars: 5g; Protein: 38g

Beefy Quesadillas

Servings: 4 | Prep Time: 15 Minutes | Cooking Time: 45 Minutes

Ingredients:

- 2 cups grated cheddar
- 1 tsp chili powder
- ½ tsp smoked paprika
- ½ tsp ground cumin
- ½ tsp nutmeg
- ¼ tsp garlic powder
- Salt and pepper to taste
- 1 ribeye steak
- 2 tsp olive oil
- 1 red bell pepper, diced
- 1 grated carrot
- 1 green bell pepper, diced
- ½ red onion, sliced
- 1 cup corn kernels
- 3 tbsp butter, melted
- 8 tortillas

Directions:

1. Mix the chili powder, nutmeg, paprika, cumin, garlic powder, salt, and pepper in a bowl. Toss in ribeye until fully coated and let marinate covered in the fridge for 30 minutes. Preheat air fryer at 200°C/400°F. Place ribeye in the greased frying basket and bake for 6 minutes until rare, flipping once. Let rest onto a cutting board for 5 minutes before slicing thinly against the grain. Warm the olive oil in a skillet over high heat. Add in bell peppers, carrot and onion and cook for 6-8 minutes until the peppers are tender. Stir in corn. Set aside. Preheat air fryer at 175°C/350°F. Brush on one side of a tortilla lightly with melted butter. Layer ¼ beef strips, ¼ bell pepper mixture, and finally, ¼ of the grated cheese. Top with a second tortilla and lightly brush with butter on top. Repeat with the remaining ingredients. Place quesadillas, butter side down, in the frying basket and bake for 3 minutes. Cut them into 6 sections and serve.

Variations & Ingredients Tips:

- Use chicken, pork, or shrimp instead of beef for different protein options.
- Add sliced jalapeños, black beans, or diced tomatoes to the veggie mixture for extra flavor.
- Serve with salsa, guacamole, or sour cream for dipping.

Per Serving: Calories: 679; Total Fat: 44g; Saturated Fat: 22g; Cholesterol: 134mg; Sodium: 727mg; Total Carbohydrates: 40g; Dietary Fiber: 5g; Total Sugars: 6g; Protein: 33g

Balsamic London Broil

Servings: 4 | Prep Time: 25 Minutes | Cooking Time: 25 Minutes

Ingredients:

- 1.13kg top round London broil steak
- 1/4 cup coconut aminos
- 1 tbsp balsamic vinegar
- 1 tbsp olive oil
- 1 tbsp mustard
- 2 tsp maple syrup
- 2 garlic cloves, minced
- 1 tsp dried oregano
- Salt and pepper to taste
- 1/4 tsp smoked paprika
- 2 tbsp chopped red onion

Directions:

1. In a bowl, whisk together coconut aminos, vinegar, oil, mustard, syrup, garlic, oregano, salt, pepper, paprika and onions.
2. Place steak in a shallow dish and pour marinade over top. Cover and marinate for 20 minutes.
3. Preheat air fryer to 200°C/400°F.
4. Transfer steak to air fryer basket and cook for 5 minutes.
5. Flip steak and cook for 4-6 more minutes for desired doneness.
6. Let rest 5 minutes before slicing against the grain.
7. Serve warm.

Variations & Ingredients Tips:

- Use soy sauce or tamari instead of coconut aminos.
- Add crushed garlic or grated ginger to the marinade.
- Slice and serve over salad greens or cauliflower rice.

Per Serving: Calories: 370; Total Fat: 15g; Saturated Fat: 5g; Cholesterol: 135mg; Sodium: 470mg; Total Carbohydrates: 7g; Dietary Fiber: 1g; Total Sugars: 5g; Protein: 52g

Sriracha Short Ribs

Servings: 4 | Prep Time: 5 Minutes | Cooking Time: 15 Minutes

Ingredients:

- 10 g sesame seeds
- 8 pork short ribs
- 118 g soy sauce
- 59 g rice wine vinegar
- 118 g chopped onion
- 2 garlic cloves, minced
- 15 g sesame oil
- 5 g sriracha
- 4 scallions, thinly sliced
- Salt and pepper to taste

Directions:

1. Put short ribs in a resealable bag along with soy sauce, vinegar, onion, garlic, sesame oil, Sriracha, half of the scallions, salt, and pepper. Seal the bag and toss to coat. Refrigerate for one hour.
2. Preheat air fryer to 190°C/380°F. Place the short ribs in the air fryer. Bake for 8-10 minutes, flipping once until crisp. When the ribs are done, garnish with remaining scallions and sesame seeds. Serve and enjoy!

Variations & Ingredients Tips:

- Use beef short ribs or country-style pork ribs for meatier bites
- Brush the ribs with honey or brown sugar in the last few minutes of cooking for a sticky glaze
- Serve with kimchi, pickled radish and steamed rice

Per Serving: Calories: 535; Total Fat: 43g; Saturated Fat: 14g; Cholesterol: 113mg; Sodium: 2319mg; Total Carbs: 9g; Dietary Fiber: 1g; Total Sugars: 3g; Protein: 27g

Chinese-style Lamb Chops

Servings: 4 | Prep Time: 10 Minutes (plus Marinating Time) | Cooking Time: 25 Minutes

Ingredients:

- 8 lamb chops, trimmed
- 2 tablespoons scallions, sliced
- ¼ teaspoon Chinese five-spice
- 3 garlic cloves, crushed
- ½ teaspoon ginger powder
- ¼ cup dark soy sauce
- 2 teaspoons orange juice
- 3 tablespoons honey
- ½ tablespoon light brown sugar
- ¼ teaspoon red pepper flakes

Directions:

1. Season the chops with garlic, ginger, soy sauce, five-spice powder, orange juice, and honey in a bowl. Toss to coat. Cover the bowl with plastic wrap and marinate for 2 hours and up to overnight.
2. Preheat air fryer to 200°C/400°F. Remove the chops from the bowl but reserve the marinade. Place the chops in the greased frying basket and Bake for 5 minutes. Using tongs, flip the chops. Brush the lamb with the reserved marinade, then sprinkle with brown sugar and pepper flakes. Cook for another 4 minutes until brown and caramelized medium-rare. Serve with scallions on top.

Variations & Ingredients Tips:

- Use different types of meat, such as pork or chicken, for a variety of flavors and textures.
- Add some minced garlic or ginger to the marinade for extra flavor.
- Serve the lamb chops with a side of stir-fried vegetables or rice for a complete meal.

Per Serving: Calories: 380; Total Fat: 21g; Saturated Fat: 8g; Cholesterol: 105mg; Sodium: 1020mg; Total Carbs: 20g; Fiber: 0g; Sugars: 18g; Protein: 30g

Greek Pork Chops

Servings: 4 | Prep Time: 10 Minutes | Cooking Time: 30 Minutes

Ingredients:

- 3 tbsp grated Halloumi cheese
- 4 pork chops
- 1 tsp Greek seasoning
- Salt and pepper to taste
- ¼ cup all-purpose flour
- 2 tbsp bread crumbs

Directions:

1. Preheat air fryer to 190°C/380°F. Season the pork chops with Greek seasoning, salt and pepper. In a shallow bowl, add flour. In another shallow bowl, combine the crumbs and Halloumi. Dip the chops in the flour, then in the bread crumbs. Place them in the fryer and spray with cooking oil. Bake for 12-14 minutes, flipping once. Serve warm.

Variations & Ingredients Tips:

- Use feta cheese instead of Halloumi for a tangier flavor
- Add some dried herbs like oregano or thyme to the breading mixture
- Serve with a Greek salad and lemon potatoes

Per Serving: Calories: 277; Total Fat: 14g; Saturated Fat: 6g; Cholesterol: 80mg; Sodium: 417mg; Total Carbs: 10g; Dietary Fiber: 0g; Total Sugars: 0g; Protein: 28g

Tender Steak With Salsa Verde

Servings: 4 | Prep Time: 10 Minutes | Cooking Time: 20 Minutes

Ingredients:

- 1 flank steak (around 680g), halved
- 1 1/2 cups salsa verde
- 1/2 tsp black pepper

Directions:

1. Toss steak and 1 cup of salsa verde in a bowl and refrigerate covered for 2 hours.
2. Preheat air fryer to 400°F/205°C.
3. Add steaks to the lightly greased frying basket and Air Fry for 10-12 minutes or until you reach your desired doneness, flipping once.
4. Let sit onto a cutting board for 5 minutes.
5. Thinly slice against the grain and divide between 4 plates.
6. Spoon over the remaining salsa verde and serve sprinkled with black pepper.

Variations & Ingredients Tips:

- Use skirt or hanger steak instead of flank steak
- Make your own salsa verde for fresher flavor
- Add sliced avocado or crumbled queso fresco as a topping

Per Serving: Calories: 250; Total Fat: 14g; Saturated Fat: 4g; Cholesterol: 65mg; Sodium: 300mg; Total Carbs: 2g; Dietary Fiber: 1g; Total Sugars: 1g; Protein: 27g

Albóndigas

Servings: 4 | Prep Time: 10 Minutes | Cooking Time: 15 Minutes

Ingredients:

- 450 g lean ground pork

- 3 tablespoons very finely chopped trimmed scallions
- 3 tablespoons finely chopped fresh cilantro leaves
- 3 tablespoons plain panko bread crumbs (gluten-free, if a concern)
- 3 tablespoons dry white wine, dry sherry, or unsweetened apple juice
- 1½ teaspoons minced garlic
- 1¼ teaspoons mild smoked paprika
- ¾ teaspoon dried oregano
- ¾ teaspoon table salt
- ¼ teaspoon ground black pepper
- Olive oil spray

Directions:

1. Preheat the air fryer to 200°C/400°F.
2. Mix the ground pork, scallions, cilantro, bread crumbs, wine or its substitute, garlic, smoked paprika, oregano, salt, and pepper in a bowl until the herbs and spices are evenly distributed in the mixture.
3. Lightly coat your clean hands with olive oil spray, then form the ground pork mixture into balls, using 2 tablespoons for each one. Spray your hands frequently so that the meat mixture doesn't stick.
4. Set the balls in the basket so that they're not touching, even if they're close together. Air-fry undisturbed for 15 minutes, or until well browned and an instant-read meat thermometer inserted into one or two balls registers 75°C/165°F.
5. Use a nonstick-safe spatula and kitchen tongs for balance to gently transfer the fragile balls to a wire rack to cool for 5 minutes before serving.

Variations & Ingredients Tips:

- Use ground beef or lamb instead of pork for a different flavor profile.
- Add some finely chopped jalapeño or red pepper flakes to the meat mixture for a spicy kick.
- Serve the albóndigas with a dipping sauce, such as romesco or aioli, for extra flavor.

Per Serving: Calories: 290; Total Fat: 18g; Saturated Fat: 6g; Cholesterol: 85mg; Sodium: 550mg; Total Carbs: 7g; Fiber: 1g; Sugars: 1g; Protein: 25g

Classic Salisbury Steak Burgers

Servings: 4 | Prep Time: 15 Minutes | Cooking Time: 35 Minutes

Ingredients:

- ¼ cup bread crumbs
- 2 tablespoons beef broth
- 1 tablespoon cooking sherry
- 1 tablespoon ketchup
- 1 tablespoon Dijon mustard
- 2 teaspoons Worcestershire sauce
- ½ teaspoon onion powder
- ½ teaspoon garlic powder
- 450 g ground beef
- 1 cup sliced mushrooms
- 1 tablespoon butter
- 4 buns, split and toasted

Directions:

1. Preheat the air fryer to 190°C/375°F.
2. Combine the bread crumbs, broth, cooking sherry, ketchup, mustard, Worcestershire sauce, garlic and onion powder and mix well. Add the beef and mix with hands, then form into 4 patties and refrigerate while preparing the mushrooms.
3. Mix the mushrooms and butter in a 15 cm pan. Place the pan in the air fryer and Bake for 8-10 minutes, stirring once until the mushrooms are brown and tender. Remove and set aside.
4. Line the frying basket with round parchment paper and punch holes in it. Lay the burgers in a single layer and cook for 11-14 minutes or until cooked through.
5. Put the burgers on the bun bottoms, top with the mushrooms, then the bun tops.

Variations & Ingredients Tips:

- Use different types of mushrooms, such as shiitake or cremini, for a variety of flavors and textures.
- Add some sliced onions or bell peppers to the mushroom mixture for extra vegetables.
- Serve the Salisbury steak burgers with a side of mashed potatoes or green beans for a classic comfort food meal.

Per Serving: Calories: 430; Total Fat: 23g; Saturated Fat: 9g; Cholesterol: 105mg; Sodium: 670mg; Total Carbs: 26g; Fiber: 2g; Sugars: 5g; Protein: 31g

Crunchy Fried Pork Loin Chops

Servings: 3 | Prep Time: 15 Minutes | Cooking Time: 12 Minutes

Ingredients:

- 1 cup all-purpose flour or tapioca flour
- 1 large egg(s), well beaten
- 1½ cups seasoned Italian-style dried bread crumbs (gluten-free, if a concern)
- 3 boneless center-cut pork loin chops (115 to 140 g each)
- Vegetable oil spray

Directions:

1. Preheat the air fryer to 180°C/350°F.
2. Set up and fill three shallow soup plates or small pie plates on your counter: one for the flour, one for the beaten egg(s), and one for the bread crumbs.
3. Dredge a pork chop in the flour, coating both sides as well as around the edge. Gently shake off any excess, then dip the chop in the egg(s), again coating both sides and the edge. Let any excess egg slip back into the rest, then set the chop in the bread crumbs, turning it and pressing gently to coat well on both sides and the edge. Coat the pork chop all over with vegetable oil spray and set aside so you can dredge, coat, and spray the additional chop(s).
4. Set the chops in the basket with as much air space between them as possible. Air-fry undisturbed for 12 minutes, or until brown and crunchy and an instant-read meat thermometer inserted into the center of a chop registers 65°C/145°F.
5. Use kitchen tongs to transfer the chops to a wire rack. Cool for 5 minutes before serving.

Variations & Ingredients Tips:

- Use different types of seasoning, such as herbs de Provence or Cajun seasoning, for a variety of flavors.
- Add some grated Parmesan cheese or nutritional yeast to the breadcrumb mixture for a cheesy flavor.
- Serve the pork chops with a side of mashed potatoes or roasted vegetables for a complete meal.

Per Serving: Calories: 430; Total Fat: 15g; Saturated Fat: 4g; Cholesterol: 145mg; Sodium: 670mg; Total Carbs: 39g; Fiber: 2g; Sugars: 3g; Protein: 37g

Fish And Seafood Recipes

Beer-breaded Halibut Fish Tacos

Servings: 4 | Prep Time: 40 Minutes | Cooking Time: 10 Minutes

Ingredients:

- 450g halibut, cut into 2.5-cm strips
- 1 cup light beer
- 1 jalapeño, minced and divided
- 1 clove garlic, minced
- 1/4 teaspoon ground cumin
- ½ cup cornmeal
- ¼ cup all-purpose flour
- 1¼ teaspoons sea salt, divided
- 2 cups shredded cabbage
- 1 lime, juiced and divided
- ¼ cup Greek yogurt
- ¼ cup Greek yogurt
- 1 cup grape tomatoes, quartered
- ½ cup chopped cilantro
- ¼ cup chopped onion
- 1 egg, whisked
- 8 corn tortillas

Directions:

1. In a shallow baking dish, place the fish, the beer, 1 teaspoon of the minced jalapeño, the garlic, and the cumin. Cover and refrigerate for 30 minutes.
2. Meanwhile, in a medium bowl, mix together the cornmeal, flour, and 1/2 teaspoon of the salt.
3. In large bowl, mix together the shredded cabbage, 1 tablespoon of the lime juice, the Greek yogurt, the may-

onnaise, and 1/2 teaspoon of the salt.
4. In a small bowl, make the pico de gallo by mixing together the tomatoes, cilantro, onion, 1/4 teaspoon of the salt, the remaining jalapeño, and the remaining lime juice.
5. Remove the fish from the refrigerator and discard the marinade. Dredge the fish in the whisked egg; then dredge the fish in the cornmeal flour mixture, until all pieces of fish have been breaded.
6. Preheat the air fryer to 175°C/350°F.
7. Place the fish in the air fryer basket and spray liberally with cooking spray. Cook for 6 minutes, flip and shake the fish, and cook another 4 minutes.
8. While the fish is cooking, heat the tortillas in a heavy skillet for 1 to 2 minutes over high heat.
9. To assemble the tacos, place the battered fish on the heated tortillas, and top with slaw and pico de gallo. Serve immediately.

Variations & Ingredients Tips:

- Use cod, tilapia or snapper instead of halibut.
- Substitute the beer with sparkling water or ginger ale for a non-alcoholic version.
- Add some sliced avocado or guacamole on top.

Per Serving: Calories: 420; Total Fat: 18g; Saturated Fat: 4g; Cholesterol: 120mg; Sodium: 910mg; Total Carbs: 37g; Dietary Fiber: 5g; Total Sugars: 5g; Protein: 29g

Sardinas Fritas

Servings: 2 | Prep Time: 5 Minutes | Cooking Time: 15 Minutes

Ingredients:

- 2 (120g) cans boneless, skinless sardines in mustard sauce
- Salt and pepper to taste
- 1/2 cup bread crumbs
- 2 lemon wedges
- 1 tsp chopped parsley

Directions:

1. Preheat air fryer at 175°C/350°F.
2. Add breadcrumbs, salt and black pepper to a bowl.
3. Roll sardines in the breadcrumbs to coat.
4. Place them in the greased frying basket and Air Fry for 6 minutes, flipping once.
5. Transfer them to a serving dish. Top with parsley and serve with lemon wedges.

Variations & Ingredients Tips:

- Use panko breadcrumbs for extra crunch.
- Add dried herbs or spices to the breadcrumb mixture.
- Serve with a remoulade or tartar sauce for dipping.

Per Serving: Calories: 310; Total Fat: 14g; Saturated Fat: 3g; Cholesterol: 135mg; Sodium: 830mg; Total Carbs: 25g; Dietary Fiber: 1g; Sugars: 1g; Protein: 22g

Salmon Puttanesca En Papillotte With Zucchini

Servings: 2 | Prep Time: 15 Minutes | Cooking Time: 17 Minutes

Ingredients:

- 1 small zucchini, sliced into 6mm thick half moons
- 1 teaspoon olive oil
- Salt and freshly ground black pepper
- 2 (140g) salmon fillets
- 1 beefsteak tomato, chopped (about 1 cup)
- 1 tablespoon capers, rinsed
- 10 black olives, pitted and sliced
- 2 tablespoons dry vermouth or white wine
- 2 tablespoons butter
- 1/4 cup chopped fresh basil

Directions:

1. Preheat air fryer to 200°C/400°F.
2. Toss zucchini with oil, salt & pepper. Air-fry 5 mins, shaking once.
3. Cut 2 (33x38cm) parchment rectangles. Divide zucchini between, place in center.
4. Top each with a salmon fillet. Season fish well with salt & pepper.
5. Toss tomato, capers, olives, vermouth; divide over fish. Top each with 1 tbsp butter.
6. Fold parchment into packets, leaving space above fish. Twist ends together.
7. Air-fry packets at 200°C/400°F for 12 mins until puffed.
8. Let sit 2 mins, then serve garnished with basil.

Variations & Ingredients Tips:

- Use other veggies like asparagus or bell peppers.
- Add white wine or chicken broth to the filling.
- Finish with a squeeze of lemon juice.

Per Serving: Calories: 450; Total Fat: 27g; Saturated Fat: 10g; Cholesterol: 95mg; Sodium: 570mg; Total Carbs: 19g; Dietary Fiber: 3g; Sugars: 6g; Protein: 30g

Panko-breaded Cod Fillets

Servings: 2 | Prep Time: 10 Minutes | Cooking Time: 20 Minutes

Ingredients:

- 1 lemon wedge, juiced and zested
- 1/2 cup panko bread crumbs
- Salt to taste
- 1 tbsp Dijon mustard
- 1 tbsp butter, melted
- 2 cod fillets

Directions:

1. Preheat air fryer to 175°C/350°F.
2. Combine all ingredients, except for the fish, in a bowl.
3. Press mixture evenly across tops of cod fillets.
4. Place fillets in the greased frying basket and Air Fry for 10 minutes until the cod is opaque and flakes easily with a fork.
5. Serve immediately.

Variations & Ingredients Tips:

- Use other white fish like haddock or pollock.
- Add grated parmesan or breadcrumbs to the panko coating.
- Serve with lemon wedges and tartar sauce.

Per Serving: Calories: 240; Total Fat: 7g; Saturated Fat: 3g; Cholesterol: 70mg; Sodium: 460mg; Total Carbs: 14g; Dietary Fiber: 1g; Sugars: 1g; Protein: 28g

Garlicky Sea Bass With Root Veggies

Servings: 4 | Prep Time: 10 Minutes | Cooking Time: 25 Minutes

Ingredients:

- 1 carrot, diced
- 1 parsnip, diced
- 1/2 rutabaga, diced
- 1/2 turnip, diced
- 1/4 cup olive oil
- Celery salt to taste
- 4 sea bass fillets
- 1/2 tsp onion powder
- 2 garlic cloves, minced
- 1 lemon, sliced

Directions:

1. Preheat air fryer to 190°C/380°F.
2. Coat the carrot, parsnip, turnip and rutabaga with olive oil and salt in a small bowl.
3. Lightly season the sea bass with and onion powder, then place into the frying basket. Spread the garlic over the top of the fillets, then cover with lemon slices.
4. Pour the prepared vegetables into the basket around and on top of the fish.
5. Roast for 15 minutes. Serve and enjoy!

Variations & Ingredients Tips:

- Use cod, halibut or snapper instead of sea bass.
- Add some fresh herbs like thyme, rosemary or dill to the vegetables.
- Serve over quinoa, couscous or rice pilaf.

Per Serving: Calories: 340; Total Fat: 19g; Saturated Fat: 3g; Cholesterol: 70mg; Sodium: 200mg; Total Carbs: 11g; Dietary Fiber: 3g; Total Sugars: 4g; Protein: 32g

Hot Calamari Rings

Servings: 4 | Prep Time: 15 Minutes | Cooking Time: 25 Minutes

Ingredients:

- 1/2 cup all-purpose flour
- 2 tsp hot chili powder
- 2 eggs
- 1 tbsp milk
- 1 cup bread crumbs
- Salt and pepper to taste
- 450g calamari rings
- 1 lime, quartered
- 1/2 cup aioli sauce

Directions:

1. Preheat air fryer at 200°C/400°F.
2. In one bowl, mix flour and chili powder.
3. In another bowl, whisk eggs and milk.
4. In a third bowl, mix breadcrumbs, salt and pepper.
5. Dredge calamari in flour, then egg, then breadcrumbs to coat.
6. Place in greased air fryer basket and cook for 4 mins,

tossing once.
7. Squeeze lime over calamari and serve with aioli sauce.

Variations & Ingredients Tips:

- Add parmesan or lemon zest to the breadcrumb mixture.
- Use panko breadcrumbs for extra crunch.
- Serve with marinara sauce instead of aioli.

Per Serving: Calories: 283; Total Fat: 10g; Saturated Fat: 2g; Cholesterol: 188mg; Sodium: 540mg; Total Carbs: 29g; Dietary Fiber: 1g; Total Sugars: 2g; Protein: 19g

Lemon & Herb Crusted Salmon

Servings: 4 | Prep Time: 10 Minutes | Cooking Time: 20 Minutes

Ingredients:

- 1/3 cup crushed potato chips
- 4 skinless salmon fillets
- 3 tbsp honey mustard
- 1/2 tsp lemon zest
- 1/2 tsp dried thyme
- 1/2 tsp dried basil
- 1/4 cup panko bread crumbs
- 2 tbsp olive oil

Directions:

1. Preheat air fryer to 160°C/320°F.
2. Place the salmon on a work surface. Mix together mustard, lemon zest, thyme, and basil in a small bowl. Spread on top of the salmon evenly.
3. In a separate small bowl, mix together bread crumbs and potato chips before drizzling with olive oil.
4. Place the salmon in the frying basket. Bake until the salmon is cooked through and the topping is crispy and brown, about 10 minutes.
5. Serve hot and enjoy!

Variations & Ingredients Tips:

- Use Dijon or whole grain mustard instead of honey mustard.
- Add some grated parmesan or pecorino to the crust mixture.
- Serve with a side of roasted potatoes and sautéed spinach.

Per Serving: Calories: 400; Total Fat: 25g; Saturated Fat: 4.5g; Cholesterol: 85mg; Sodium: 280mg; Total Carbs: 12g; Dietary Fiber: 1g; Total Sugars: 3g; Protein: 32g

Tilapia Al Pesto

Servings: 4 | Prep Time: 15 Minutes | Cooking Time: 25 Minutes

Ingredients:

- 4 tilapia fillets
- 1 egg
- 2 tbsp buttermilk
- 1 cup crushed cornflakes
- Salt and pepper to taste
- 4 tsp pesto
- 2 tbsp butter, melted
- 4 lemon wedges

Directions:

1. Preheat air fryer to 175°C/350°F.
2. Whisk egg and buttermilk in a bowl. In another bowl, combine cornflakes, salt, and pepper.
3. Spread 1 tsp of pesto on each tilapia fillet, then tightly roll the fillet from one short end to the other. Secure with a toothpick.
4. Dip each fillet in the egg mixture and dredge in the cornflake mixture. Place fillets in the greased frying basket, drizzle with melted butter, and Air Fry for 6 minutes.
5. Let rest onto a serving dish for 5 minutes before removing the toothpicks.
6. Serve with lemon wedges.

Variations & Ingredients Tips:

- Use cod, sole or flounder instead of tilapia.
- Substitute pesto with sun-dried tomato paste or olive tapenade.
- Serve over a bed of sautéed spinach or roasted vegetables.

Per Serving: Calories: 320; Total Fat: 16g; Saturated Fat: 6g; Cholesterol: 110mg; Sodium: 400mg; Total Carbs: 18g; Dietary Fiber: 1g; Total Sugars: 2g; Protein: 28g

Summer Sea Scallops

Servings: 4 | Prep Time: 10 Minutes | Cooking Time: 30 Minutes

Ingredients:

- 1 cup asparagus
- 1 cup peas
- 1 cup chopped broccoli
- 2 tsp olive oil
- ½ tsp dried oregano
- 340g sea scallops

Directions:

1. Preheat air fryer to 200°C/400°F.
2. Add the asparagus, peas, and broccoli to a bowl and mix with olive oil.
3. Put the bowl in the fryer and Air Fry for 4-6 minutes until crispy and soft. Take the veggies out and add the herbs; let sit.
4. Add the scallops to the fryer and Air Fry for 4-5 minutes until the scallops are springy to the touch.
5. Serve immediately with the vegetables. Enjoy!

Variations & Ingredients Tips:

- Use green beans, zucchini or cherry tomatoes instead of broccoli.
- Toss the vegetables with lemon juice and garlic for extra flavor.
- Serve over a bed of quinoa, couscous or pasta.

Per Serving: Calories: 180; Total Fat: 4g; Saturated Fat: 0.5g; Cholesterol: 50mg; Sodium: 880mg; Total Carbs: 12g; Dietary Fiber: 3g; Total Sugars: 4g; Protein: 24g

The Best Oysters Rockefeller

Servings: 2 | Prep Time: 20 Minutes | Cooking Time: 30 Minutes

Ingredients:

- 4 tsp grated Parmesan
- 2 tbsp butter
- 1 sweet onion, minced
- 1 clove garlic, minced
- 1 cup baby spinach
- 1/8 tsp Tabasco hot sauce
- 1/2 tsp lemon juice
- 1/2 tsp lemon zest
- 1/4 cup bread crumbs
- 12 oysters, on the half shell

Directions:

1. Melt butter in a skillet over medium heat. Stir in onion, garlic, and spinach and stir-fry for 3 minutes until the onion is translucent. Mix in Parmesan cheese, hot sauce, lemon juice, lemon zest, and bread crumbs. Divide this mixture between the tops of oysters.
2. Preheat air fryer to 200°C/400°F. Place oysters in the frying basket and Air Fry for 6 minutes.
3. Serve immediately.

Variations & Ingredients Tips:

- Substitute spinach with kale, arugula or watercress.
- Add some crispy bacon bits or pancetta to the topping.
- Serve with lemon wedges and hot sauce on the side.

Per Serving: Calories: 370; Total Fat: 25g; Saturated Fat: 13g; Cholesterol: 125mg; Sodium: 510mg; Total Carbs: 21g; Dietary Fiber: 2g; Total Sugars: 4g; Protein: 17g

Tuna Nuggets In Hoisin Sauce

Servings: 4 | Prep Time: 10 Minutes | Cooking Time: 7 Minutes

Ingredients:

- 1/2 cup hoisin sauce
- 2 tablespoons rice wine vinegar
- 2 teaspoons sesame oil
- 1 teaspoon garlic powder
- 2 teaspoons dried lemongrass
- 1/4 teaspoon red pepper flakes
- 1/2 small onion, quartered and thinly sliced
- 225g fresh tuna, cut into 2.5-cm cubes
- Cooking spray
- 3 cups cooked jasmine rice

Directions:

1. Mix the hoisin sauce, vinegar, sesame oil, and seasonings together.
2. Stir in the onions and tuna nuggets.
3. Spray air fryer baking pan with nonstick spray and pour in tuna mixture.
4. Cook at 200°C/390°F for 3 minutes. Stir gently.
5. Cook 2 minutes and stir again, checking for doneness. Tuna should be barely cooked through, just beginning to flake and still very moist. If necessary, continue cooking and stirring in 1-minute intervals until done.
6. Serve warm over hot jasmine rice.

Variations & Ingredients Tips:

- Use salmon, swordfish or shrimp instead of tuna.
- Add some diced bell peppers or carrots to the mix.
- Serve over rice noodles or in lettuce wraps.

Per Serving: Calories: 350; Total Fat: 6g; Saturated Fat: 1g; Cholesterol: 30mg; Sodium: 950mg; Total Carbs: 54g; Dietary Fiber: 2g; Total Sugars: 13g; Protein: 22g

Chinese Fish Noodle Bowls

Servings: 4 | Prep Time: 25 Minutes | Cooking Time: 40 Minutes

Ingredients:

- 1 can crushed pineapple, drained
- 1 shallot, minced
- 2 tbsp chopped cilantro
- 2 1/2 tsp lime juice
- 1 tbsp honey
- Salt and pepper to taste
- 1 1/2 cups grated red cabbage
- 1/4 cup chopped green beans
- 2 grated baby carrots
- 1/2 tsp granulated sugar
- 2 tbsp mayonnaise
- 1 clove garlic, minced
- 225g cooked rice noodles
- 2 tsp sesame oil
- 1 tsp sesame seeds
- 4 cod fillets
- 1 tsp Chinese five-spice

Directions:

1. Preheat air fryer at 175°C/350°F.
2. Combine the pineapple, shallot, 1 tbsp of cilantro, honey, 2 tsp of lime juice, salt, and black pepper in a bowl. Let chill the salsa covered in the fridge until ready to use.
3. Mix the cabbage, green beans, carrots, sugar, remaining lime juice, mayonnaise, garlic, salt, and pepper in a bowl. Let chill covered in the fridge until ready to use.
4. In a bowl, toss cooked noodles and sesame oil, stirring occasionally to avoid sticking.
5. Sprinkle cod fillets with salt and five-spice. Place them in the greased frying basket and Air Fry for 10 minutes until the fish is opaque and flakes easily with a fork.
6. Divide noodles into 4 bowls, top each with salsa, slaw, and fish. Serve right away sprinkled with another tbsp of cilantro and sesame seeds.

Variations & Ingredients Tips:

- Use salmon, shrimp or tofu instead of cod.
- Add some sliced mango or papaya to the salsa.
- Drizzle with a spicy Sriracha mayo sauce.

Per Serving: Calories: 400; Total Fat: 13g; Saturated Fat: 2g; Cholesterol: 65mg; Sodium: 330mg; Total Carbs: 45g; Dietary Fiber: 4g; Total Sugars: 18g; Protein: 27g

Spiced Salmon Croquettes

Servings: 6 | Prep Time: 10 Minutes | Cooking Time: 20 Minutes

Ingredients:

- 1 (210g) can Alaskan pink salmon, bones removed
- 1 lime, zested
- 1 red chili, minced
- 2 tbsp cilantro, chopped
- 1 egg, beaten
- 1/2 cup bread crumbs
- 2 scallions, diced
- 1 tsp garlic powder
- Salt and pepper to taste

Directions:

1. Preheat air fryer to 200°C/400°F.
2. Mix salmon, egg, crumbs, scallions in a bowl.
3. Add garlic, lime zest, chili, cilantro, salt & pepper.
4. Divide into 6 portions and shape into patties.
5. Place patties in greased air fryer basket.
6. Air Fry 7 minutes, flip and cook 4 more mins until golden.
7. Serve.

Variations & Ingredients Tips:

- Use fresh or canned salmon.
- Add diced red bell pepper or jalapeño.
- Substitute panko crumbs for extra crunch.

Per Serving: Calories: 140; Total Fat: 4g; Saturated Fat: 1g; Cholesterol: 70mg; Sodium: 380mg; Total Carbs: 12g; Dietary Fiber: 1g; Sugars: 1g; Protein: 13g

Sweet & Spicy Swordfish Kebabs

Servings: 4 | Prep Time: 15 Minutes | Cooking Time: 30 Minutes

Ingredients:

- ½ cup canned pineapple chunks, drained, juice reserved
- 453g swordfish steaks, cubed
- ½ cup large red grapes
- 1 tbsp honey
- 2 tsp grated fresh ginger
- 1 tsp olive oil
- Pinch cayenne pepper

Directions:

1. Preheat air fryer to 190°C/370°F.
2. Poke 8 bamboo skewers through the swordfish, pineapple, and grapes.
3. Mix the honey, 1 tbsp of pineapple juice, ginger, olive oil, and cayenne in a bowl, then use a brush to rub the mix on the kebabs. Allow the marinade to sit on the kebabs for 10 minutes.
4. Grill the kebabs for 8-12 minutes until the fish is cooked through and the fruit is soft and glazed. Brush the kebabs again with the mix, then toss the rest of the marinade.
5. Serve warm and enjoy!

Variations & Ingredients Tips:

- Use mango or peach chunks instead of pineapple for a different tropical flavor.
- Add some red bell pepper pieces to the skewers for color and crunch.
- Sprinkle with chopped cilantro or mint before serving for freshness.

Per Serving: Calories: 220; Total Fat: 5g; Saturated Fat: 1g; Cholesterol: 65mg; Sodium: 180mg; Total Carbohydrates: 15g; Dietary Fiber: 1g; Total Sugars: 12g; Protein: 28g

Catfish Nuggets

Servings: 4 | Prep Time: 15 Minutes | Cooking Time: 7 Minutes Per Batch

Ingredients:

- 2 medium catfish fillets, cut in chunks (approximately 2.5 x 5 cm)
- salt and pepper
- 2 eggs
- 2 tablespoons skim milk
- ½ cup cornstarch
- 1 cup panko breadcrumbs, crushed
- oil for misting or cooking spray

Directions:

1. Season catfish chunks with salt and pepper to your liking.
2. Beat together eggs and milk in a small bowl.
3. Place cornstarch in a second small bowl.
4. Place breadcrumbs in a third small bowl.
5. Dip catfish chunks in cornstarch, dip in egg wash, shake off excess, then roll in breadcrumbs.
6. Spray all sides of catfish chunks with oil or cooking spray.
7. Place chunks in air fryer basket in a single layer, leaving space between for air circulation.
8. Cook at 200°C/390°F for 4 minutes, turn, and cook an additional 3 minutes, until fish flakes easily and outside is crispy brown.
9. Repeat steps 7 and 8 to cook remaining catfish nuggets.

Variations & Ingredients Tips:

- Use cod, tilapia, or halibut instead of catfish for different fish options.
- Add garlic powder, onion powder, or Old Bay seasoning to the breading mix for extra flavor.
- Serve with tartar sauce, remoulade, or cocktail sauce for dipping.

Per Serving: Calories: 280; Total Fat: 9g; Saturated Fat: 2g; Sodium: 420mg; Total Carbohydrates: 25g; Dietary Fiber: 1g; Total Sugars: 2g; Protein: 24g

Timeless Garlic-lemon Scallops

Servings: 2 | Prep Time: 5 Minutes | Cooking Time: 15 Minutes

Ingredients:

- 2 tbsp butter, melted
- 1 garlic clove, minced
- 1 tbsp lemon juice
- 450g jumbo sea scallops

Directions:

53

1. Preheat air fryer to 200°C/400°F.
2. Whisk butter, garlic, and lemon juice in a bowl. Roll scallops in the mixture to coat all sides.
3. Place scallops in the frying basket and Air Fry for 4 minutes, flipping once. Brush the tops of each scallop with butter mixture and cook for 4 more minutes, flipping once.
4. Serve and enjoy!

Variations & Ingredients Tips:

- Sprinkle scallops with Old Bay seasoning or smoked paprika.
- Wrap each scallop with a slice of prosciutto before air frying.
- Serve over angel hair pasta or creamy risotto.

Per Serving: Calories: 290; Total Fat: 16g; Saturated Fat: 9g; Cholesterol: 100mg; Sodium: 990mg; Total Carbs: 5g; Dietary Fiber: 0g; Total Sugars: 0g; Protein: 33g

Beer-battered Cod

Servings: 3 | Prep Time: 15 Minutes | Cooking Time: 12 Minutes

Ingredients:

- 1½ cups All-purpose flour
- 3 tablespoons Old Bay seasoning
- 1 large egg
- ¼ cup Amber beer, pale ale, or IPA
- 3 (115g) skinless cod fillets
- Vegetable oil spray

Directions:

1. Preheat the air fryer to 200°C/400°F.
2. Set up and fill two shallow soup plates or small pie plates on your counter: one with the flour, whisked with the Old Bay until well combined; and one with the egg, whisked with the beer until foamy and uniform.
3. Dip a piece of cod in the flour mixture, turning it to coat on all sides (not just the top and bottom). Gently shake off any excess flour and dip the fish in the egg mixture, turning it to coat. Let any excess egg mixture slip back into the rest, then set the fish back in the flour mixture and coat it again, then back in the egg mixture for a second wash, then back in the flour mixture for a third time. Coat the fish on all sides with vegetable oil spray and set it aside. "Batter" the remaining piece(s) of cod in the same way.
4. Set the coated cod fillets in the basket with as much space between them as possible. They should not touch. Air-fry undisturbed for 12 minutes, or until brown and crisp.
5. Use kitchen tongs to gently transfer the fish to a wire rack. Cool for only a couple of minutes before serving.

Variations & Ingredients Tips:

- Use haddock, pollack or catfish instead of cod.
- Substitute beer with sparkling water for a non-alcoholic version.
- Serve with french fries, coleslaw and malt vinegar.

Per Serving: Calories: 330; Total Fat: 5g; Saturated Fat: 1g; Cholesterol: 115mg; Sodium: 1120mg; Total Carbs: 44g; Dietary Fiber: 2g; Total Sugars: 1g; Protein: 26g

Kid's Flounder Fingers

Servings: 4 | Prep Time: 10 Minutes | Cooking Time: 45 Minutes

Ingredients:

- 450g catfish flounder fillets, cut into 2.5cm chunks
- 1/2 cup seasoned fish fry breading mix

Directions:

1. Preheat air fryer to 200°C/400°F.
2. In a resealable bag, add flounder chunks and breading mix.
3. Seal and shake bag until fish is coated.
4. Place coated nuggets in a single layer in greased air fryer basket.
5. Air fry for 18-20 minutes, shaking basket once, until crisp.
6. Serve warm.

Variations & Ingredients Tips:

- Use any firm white fish like cod or haddock.
- Make your own seasoned breadcrumb mix with spices.
- Serve with tartar sauce, ketchup or ranch for dipping.

Per Serving: Calories: 167; Total Fat: 2g; Saturated Fat: 0g; Cholesterol: 51mg; Sodium: 513mg; Total Carbs: 13g; Dietary Fiber: 0g; Total Sugars: 1g; Protein: 23g

Californian Tilapia

Servings: 4 | Prep Time: 10 Minutes | Cooking

Time: 15 Minutes

Ingredients:

- Salt and pepper to taste
- ¼ tsp garlic powder
- ¼ tsp chili powder
- ¼ tsp dried oregano
- ¼ tsp smoked paprika
- 1 tbsp butter, melted
- 4 tilapia fillets
- 2 tbsp lime juice
- 1 lemon, sliced

Directions:

1. Preheat air fryer to 200°C/400°F.
2. Combine salt, pepper, oregano, garlic powder, chili powder, and paprika in a small bowl.
3. Place tilapia in a pie pan, then pour lime juice and butter over the fish. Season both sides of the fish with the spice blend.
4. Arrange the tilapia in a single layer of the parchment-lined air fryer basket without touching each other.
5. Air Fry for 4 minutes, then carefully flip the fish. Air Fry for another 4 to 5 minutes until the fish is cooked and the outside is crispy.
6. Serve immediately with lemon slices on the side and enjoy.

Variations & Ingredients Tips:

- Substitute tilapia with cod, halibut, or snapper fillets.
- Add a sprinkle of grated Parmesan cheese or panko breadcrumbs before air frying for a crispy crust.
- Serve with avocado slices, pico de gallo, or a side of black beans and rice.

Per Serving: Calories: 160; Total Fat: 6g; Saturated Fat: 3g; Sodium: 200mg; Total Carbohydrates: 2g; Dietary Fiber: 0g; Total Sugars: 0g; Protein: 24g

Maple Balsamic Glazed Salmon

Servings: 4 | Prep Time: 5 Minutes | Cooking Time: 10 Minutes

Ingredients:

- 4 (170g) fillets of salmon
- Salt and freshly ground black pepper
- Vegetable oil
- 1/4 cup pure maple syrup
- 3 tablespoons balsamic vinegar
- 1 teaspoon Dijon mustard

Directions:

1. Preheat the air fryer to 200°C/400°F.
2. Season the salmon well with salt and freshly ground black pepper. Spray or brush the bottom of the air fryer basket with vegetable oil and place the salmon fillets inside. Air-fry the salmon for 5 minutes.
3. While the salmon is air-frying, combine the maple syrup, balsamic vinegar and Dijon mustard in a small saucepan over medium heat and stir to blend well. Let the mixture simmer while the fish is cooking. It should start to thicken slightly, but keep your eye on it so it doesn't burn.
4. Brush the glaze on the salmon fillets and air-fry for an additional 5 minutes. The salmon should feel firm to the touch when finished and the glaze should be nicely browned on top. Brush a little more glaze on top before removing and serving with rice and vegetables, or a nice green salad.

Variations & Ingredients Tips:

- Substitute honey for the maple syrup if desired.
- Add a pinch of red pepper flakes to the glaze for some heat.
- Garnish with fresh thyme or parsley before serving.

Per Serving: Calories: 330; Total Fat: 14g; Saturated Fat: 2g; Cholesterol: 95mg; Sodium: 130mg; Total Carbs: 18g; Dietary Fiber: 0g; Total Sugars: 14g; Protein: 33g

Peppery Tilapia Roulade

Servings: 4 | Prep Time: 15 Minutes | Cooking Time: 25 Minutes

Ingredients:

- 4 jarred roasted red pepper slices
- 1 egg
- 1/2 cup breadcrumbs
- Salt and pepper to taste
- 4 tilapia fillets
- 2 tbsp butter, melted
- 4 lime wedges
- 1 tsp dill

Directions:

1. Preheat air fryer at 175°C/350°F.
2. Beat the egg and 2 tbsp of water in a bowl. In another bowl, mix the breadcrumbs, salt, and pepper.
3. Place a red pepper slice and sprinkle with dill on each fish fillet. Tightly roll tilapia fillets from one short end to the other. Secure with toothpicks.
4. Roll each fillet in the egg mixture, then dredge them in the breadcrumbs.
5. Place fish rolls in the greased frying basket and drizzle the tops with melted butter.
6. Roast for 6 minutes. Let rest in a serving dish for 5 minutes before removing the toothpicks.
7. Serve with lime wedges. Enjoy!

Variations & Ingredients Tips:

- Use sundried tomatoes or spinach instead of roasted peppers.
- Add shredded cheese or pesto to the filling.
- Serve with lemon garlic sauce for dipping.

Per Serving: Calories: 250; Total Fat: 9g; Saturated Fat: 4g; Cholesterol: 130mg; Sodium: 320mg; Total Carbs: 14g; Dietary Fiber: 1g; Sugars: 1g; Protein: 27g

Vegetarian Recipes

Chive Potato Pierogi

Servings: 4 | Prep Time: 25 Minutes | Cooking Time: 55 Minutes

Ingredients:

- 2 boiled potatoes (around 340g), mashed
- Salt and pepper to taste
- 1 tsp cumin powder
- 2 tbsp sour cream
- 1/4 cup grated Parmesan
- 2 tbsp chopped chives
- 1 tbsp chopped parsley
- 1 1/4 cups flour
- 1/4 tsp garlic powder
- 3/4 cup Greek yogurt
- 1 egg
- Cooking spray or oil for greasing

Directions:

1. Combine the mashed potatoes along with sour cream, cumin, parsley, chives, pepper, and salt and stir until slightly chunky.
2. Mix the flour, salt, and garlic powder in a large bowl. Stir in yogurt until it comes together as a sticky dough. Knead in the bowl for about 2-3 minutes to make it smooth.
3. Whisk the egg and 1 teaspoon of water in a small bowl.
4. Roll out the dough on a lightly floured work surface to 6-mm thickness. Cut out 12 circles with a cookie cutter.
5. Preheat air fryer to 175°C/350°F.
6. Divide the potato mixture and Parmesan cheese between the dough circles. Brush the edges with the egg wash and fold the dough over the filling into half-moon shapes. Crimp the edges with a fork to seal.
7. Arrange the pierogies on the greased frying basket and Air Fry for 8-10 minutes, turning once, until the outside is golden.
8. Serve warm.

Variations & Ingredients Tips:

- Add cooked bacon or caramelized onions to the potato filling for extra flavor.
- Substitute Greek yogurt with sour cream or milk in the dough if desired.
- Serve with a side of sauteed mushrooms or roasted vegetables.

Per Serving (3 pierogies): Calories: 320, Total Fat: 9g, Saturated Fat: 4g, Cholesterol: 60mg, Sodium: 310mg, Total Carbs: 46g, Dietary Fiber: 3g, Total Sugars: 3g, Protein: 12g

Lentil Burritos With Cilantro Chutney

Servings: 4 | Prep Time: 20 Minutes | Cooking Time: 30 Minutes

Ingredients:

- 1 cup cilantro chutney
- 454 grams cooked potatoes, mashed
- 2 tsp sunflower oil
- 3 garlic cloves, minced
- 1 ½ tbsp fresh lime juice
- 1 ½ tsp cumin powder
- 1 tsp onion powder
- 1 tsp coriander powder
- Salt to taste
- ½ tsp turmeric
- ¼ tsp cayenne powder
- 4 large flour tortillas
- 1 cup cooked lentils
- ½ cup shredded cabbage
- ¼ cup minced red onions

Directions:

1. Preheat air fryer to 200°C/390°F.
2. Place the mashed potatoes, sunflower oil, garlic, lime, cumin, onion powder, coriander, salt, turmeric, and cayenne in a large bowl. Stir well until combined.
3. Lay the tortillas out flat on the counter. In the middle of each, distribute the potato filling. Add some of the lentils, cabbage, and red onions on top of the potatoes.
4. Close the wraps by folding the bottom of the tortillas up and over the filling, then folding the sides in, then roll the bottom up to form a burrito.
5. Place the wraps in the greased air fryer basket, seam side down. Air Fry for 6-8 minutes, flipping once until golden and crispy.
6. Serve topped with cilantro chutney.

Variations & Ingredients Tips:

- Make your own cilantro chutney by blending fresh cilantro, mint, green chili, lime juice, and salt.
- Use kidney beans or black beans instead of lentils for variation.
- Add shredded cheese to the filling for extra richness and flavor.

Per Serving: Calories: 510; Total Fat: 13g; Saturated Fat: 2g; Sodium: 820mg; Total Carbohydrates: 87g; Dietary Fiber: 13g; Total Sugars: 6g; Protein: 18g

Cheddar Stuffed Portobellos With Salsa

Servings: 4 | Prep Time: 10 Minutes | Cooking Time: 20 Minutes

Ingredients:

- 8 portobello mushrooms
- 1/3 cup salsa
- ½ cup shredded cheddar
- 2 tbsp cilantro, chopped

Directions:

1. Preheat air fryer to 190°C/370°F. Remove the mushroom stems. Divide the salsa between the caps. Top with cheese and sprinkle with cilantro. Place the mushrooms in the greased frying basket and Bake for 8-10 minutes. Let cool slightly, then serve.

Variations & Ingredients Tips:

- Substitute cheddar with mozzarella, pepper jack, or a vegan cheese alternative.
- Add diced bell peppers, onions, or jalapeños to the salsa for extra veggies.
- Serve with sour cream, guacamole, or extra salsa on the side.

Per Serving (2 mushrooms): Calories: 120; Cholesterol: 15mg; Total Fat: 7g; Saturated Fat: 4g; Sodium: 320mg; Total Carbohydrates: 8g; Dietary Fiber: 2g; Total Sugars: 3g; Protein: 8g

Quick-to-make Quesadillas

Servings: 4 | Prep Time: 20 Minutes | Cooking Time: 30 Minutes

Ingredients:

- 340 grams goat cheese
- 2 tbsp vinegar
- 1 tbsp Taco seasoning
- 1 ripe avocado, pitted
- 4 scallions, finely sliced
- 2 tbsp lemon juice
- 4 flour tortillas
- ¼ cup hot sauce
- ½ cup Alfredo sauce
- 16 cherry tomatoes, halved

Directions:

1. Preheat air fryer to 200°C/400°F.
2. Slice goat cheese into 4 pieces. Set aside. In a bowl, whisk vinegar and taco seasoning until combined. Submerge each slice into the vinegar and Air Fry for 12 minutes until crisp, turning once. Let cool slightly before cutting into 1-cm thick strips.
3. Using a fork, mash the avocado in a bowl. Stir in scallions and lemon juice and set aside.
4. Lay one tortilla on a flat surface, cut from one edge to the center, then spread ¼ of the avocado mixture on one quadrant, 1 tbsp of hot sauce on the next quadrant, and finally 2 tbsp of Alfredo sauce on the other half. Top the non-sauce half with ¼ of cherry tomatoes and ¼ of goat cheese strips.
5. To fold, start with the avocado quadrant, folding each over the next one until you create a stacked triangle. Repeat the process with the remaining tortillas.
6. Air Fry for 5 minutes until crispy, turning once. Serve warm.

Variations & Ingredients Tips:

- Use feta cheese or queso fresco instead of goat cheese.
- Add sautéed bell peppers and onions to the filling.
- Serve with salsa, sour cream, or guacamole for dipping.

Per Serving: Calories: 500; Total Fat: 28g; Saturated Fat: 17g; Sodium: 1050mg; Total Carbohydrates: 42g; Dietary Fiber: 5g; Total Sugars: 6g; Protein: 22g

Falafels

Servings: 12 | Prep Time: 10 Minutes | Cooking Time: 10 Minutes

Ingredients:

- 1 pouch falafel mix
- 2–3 tablespoons plain breadcrumbs
- Oil for misting or cooking spray

Directions:

1. Prepare falafel mix according to package directions.
2. Preheat air fryer to 200°C/390°F.
3. Place breadcrumbs in shallow dish or on wax paper.
4. Shape falafel mixture into 12 balls and flatten slightly. Roll in breadcrumbs to coat all sides and mist with oil or cooking spray.
5. Place falafels in air fryer basket in single layer and cook for 5 minutes. Shake basket, and continue cooking for 5 minutes, until they brown and are crispy.

Variations & Ingredients Tips:

- Add finely chopped parsley, cilantro or mint to the falafel mix for extra flavor.
- Serve with tahini sauce, hummus or tzatziki for dipping.
- Stuff falafels in pita bread with veggies for a filling meal.

Per Serving: Calories: 50; Total Fat: 2g; Saturated Fat: 0.2g; Sodium: 100mg; Total Carbs: 6g; Dietary Fiber: 1g; Protein: 2g

Mushroom Bolognese Casserole

Servings: 4 | Prep Time: 10 Minutes | Cooking Time: 20 Minutes

Ingredients:

- 1 cup canned diced tomatoes
- 2 garlic cloves, minced
- 1 tsp onion powder
- ¾ tsp dried basil
- ¾ tsp dried oregano
- 1 cup chopped mushrooms
- 454 grams cooked spaghetti

Directions:

1. Preheat air fryer to 200°C/400°F.
2. Whisk the tomatoes and their juices, garlic, onion powder, basil, oregano, and mushrooms in a baking pan. Cover with aluminum foil and Bake for 6 minutes.
3. Slide out the pan and add the cooked spaghetti; stir to coat. Cover with aluminum foil and Bake for 3 minutes until and bubbly.
4. Serve and enjoy!

Variations & Ingredients Tips:

- Use zucchini noodles or spaghetti squash instead of regular pasta for a low-carb option.
- Add plant-based ground meat substitute for a meatier texture and more protein.
- Top with grated Parmesan cheese or nutritional yeast before serving.

Per Serving: Calories: 240; Total Fat: 1.5g; Saturated Fat: 0g; Sodium: 60mg; Total Carbohydrates: 49g; Dietary Fiber: 3g; Total Sugars: 4g; Protein: 9g

Bengali Samosa With Mango Chutney

Servings: 4 | Prep Time: 20 Minutes | Cooking Time: 65 Minutes

Ingredients:

- ¼ tsp ground fenugreek seeds
- 1 cup diced mango
- 1 tbsp minced red onion
- 2 tsp honey
- 1 tsp minced ginger
- 1 tsp apple cider vinegar
- 1 phyllo dough sheet
- 2 tbsp olive oil
- 1 potato, mashed
- ½ tsp garam masala
- ¼ tsp ground turmeric
- ⅛ tsp chili powder
- ¼ tsp ground cumin
- ½ cup green peas
- 2 scallions, chopped

Directions:

1. Mash mango in a small bowl until chunky. Stir in onion, ginger, honey, and vinegar. Save in the fridge until ready to use. Place the mashed potato in a bowl. Add half of the olive oil, garam masala, turmeric, chili powder, ground fenugreek seeds, cumin, and salt and stir until mostly smooth. Stir in peas and scallions.
2. Preheat air fryer to 220°C/425°F. Lightly flour a flat work surface and transfer the phyllo dough. Cut into 8 equal portions and roll each portion to 6-mm thick rounds. Divide the potato filling between the dough rounds. Fold in three sides and pinch at the meeting point, almost like a pyramid. Arrange the samosas in the frying basket and brush with the remaining olive oil. Bake for 10 minutes, then flip the samosas. Bake for another 4-6 minutes until the crust is crisp and golden. Serve with mango chutney.

Variations & Ingredients Tips:

▶ Use store-bought mango chutney for a quicker version.
▶ Substitute phyllo dough with puff pastry or wonton wrappers if desired.
▶ Add chopped cashews or raisins to the potato filling for extra texture and flavor.

Per Serving: Calories: 310; Cholesterol: 0mg; Total Fat: 13g; Saturated Fat: 2g; Sodium: 180mg; Total Carbohydrates: 45g; Dietary Fiber: 5g; Total Sugars: 15g; Protein: 6g

Pizza Margherita With Spinach

Servings: 4 | Prep Time: 30 Minutes | Cooking Time: 50 Minutes

Ingredients:

- ½ cup pizza sauce
- 1 tsp dried oregano
- 1 tsp garlic powder
- 1 pizza dough
- 1 cup baby spinach
- ½ cup mozzarella cheese

Directions:

1. Preheat air fryer to 200°C/400°F.
2. Whisk pizza sauce, oregano, and garlic in a bowl. Set aside.
3. Form 4 balls with the pizza dough and roll out each into a 15-cm round pizza.
4. Lay one crust in the basket, spread ¼ of the sauce, then scatter with ¼ of spinach, and finally top with mozzarella cheese.
5. Grill for 8 minutes until golden brown and the crust is crispy.
6. Repeat the process with the remaining crusts. Serve immediately.

Variations & Ingredients Tips:

▶ Add sliced cherry tomatoes, mushrooms, or bell peppers as additional toppings.
▶ Sprinkle with red pepper flakes for some heat.
▶ Brush the crust with garlic butter before adding toppings for extra flavor.

Per Serving: Calories: 280; Total Fat: 9g; Saturated Fat: 3.5g; Sodium: 520mg; Total Carbohydrates: 39g; Dietary Fiber: 2g; Total Sugars: 4g; Protein: 11g

Falafel

Servings: 4 | Prep Time: 15 Minutes | Cooking Time: 10 Minutes

Ingredients:

- One 400-gram can garbanzo beans (chick-

- peas), drained and rinsed
- 1 clove garlic, chopped
- 1 cup chopped parsley
- ½ cup chopped dill
- ½ teaspoon ground cumin
- ½ teaspoon ground coriander
- 1 teaspoon salt
- ¼ cup sesame seeds
- ½ cup breadcrumbs

Directions:

1. Preheat the air fryer to 175°C/350°F.
2. Pat the garbanzo beans dry with a towel. In a food processor, place the beans, garlic, parsley, dill, cumin, coriander, and salt. Blend for 2 minutes, scraping down the sides of the food processor every 30 seconds.
3. In a small bowl, mix together the breadcrumbs and sesame seeds. Working one at a time and using a cookie scoop or approximately 2 tablespoons, form a patty about 1.25-cm thick and round. Dredge the patties in the breadcrumb mixture.
4. Place the falafel in the air fryer basket, making sure they don't overlap. Spray with cooking spray and cook for 6 minutes, flip over, and cook another 4 to 6 minutes. Cook in batches as needed.

Variations & Ingredients Tips:

- Add diced onions, red pepper flakes, or lemon juice to the falafel mixture for extra flavor.
- Serve in a pita with lettuce, tomato, and tzatziki sauce for a classic falafel sandwich.
- Use a mixture of chickpeas and fava beans for a more authentic taste.

Per Serving (3 falafel): Calories: 250; Cholesterol: 0mg; Total Fat: 8g; Saturated Fat: 1g; Sodium: 770mg; Total Carbohydrates: 36g; Dietary Fiber: 8g; Total Sugars: 5g; Protein: 11g

Tortilla Pizza Margherita

Servings: 1 | Prep Time: 5 Minutes | Cooking Time: 15 Minutes

Ingredients:

- 1 flour tortilla
- ¼ cup tomato sauce
- 1/3 cup grated mozzarella
- 3 basil leaves

Directions:

1. Preheat air fryer to 180°C/350°F.
2. Put the tortilla in the greased basket and pour the sauce in the center. Spread across the whole tortilla.
3. Sprinkle with cheese and Bake for 8-10 minutes or until crisp.
4. Remove carefully and top with basil leaves. Serve hot.

Variations & Ingredients Tips:

- Add sliced cherry tomatoes, olives, or mushrooms as additional toppings.
- Use pesto sauce instead of tomato sauce for a green pizza.
- Sprinkle with red pepper flakes or dried oregano for extra seasoning.

Per Serving: Calories: 290; Total Fat: 12g; Saturated Fat: 5g; Sodium: 780mg; Total Carbohydrates: 31g; Dietary Fiber: 2g; Total Sugars: 4g; Protein: 14g

Zucchini Tacos

Servings: 3 | Prep Time: 10 Minutes | Cooking Time: 20 Minutes

Ingredients:

- 1 small zucchini, sliced
- 1 yellow onion, sliced
- 1/4 tsp garlic powder
- Salt and pepper to taste
- 1 can refried beans
- 6 corn tortillas, warm
- 1 cup guacamole
- 1 tbsp cilantro, chopped

Directions:

1. Preheat air fryer to 200°C/390°F.
2. Place the zucchini and onion in the greased frying basket. Spray with more oil and sprinkle with garlic, salt, and pepper to taste.
3. Roast for 6 minutes. Remove, shake, or stir, then cook for another 6 minutes, until the veggies are golden and tender.
4. In a pan, heat the refried beans over low heat. Stir often. When warm enough, remove from heat and set aside.
5. Place a corn tortilla on a plate and fill it with beans, roasted vegetables, and guacamole.
6. Top with cilantro to serve.

Variations & Ingredients Tips:

- Use flour or whole wheat tortillas instead of corn.
- Top with vegan sour cream, salsa or hot sauce.
- Add black beans or roasted sweet potatoes to the filling.

Per Serving: Calories: 275; Total Fat: 11g; Saturated Fat: 2g; Sodium: 745mg; Total Carbohydrates: 38g; Dietary Fiber: 9g; Total Sugars: 5g; Protein: 9g

Broccoli Cheddar Stuffed Potatoes

Servings: 2 | Prep Time: 15 Minutes | Cooking Time: 42 Minutes

Ingredients:

- 2 large russet potatoes, scrubbed
- 1 tablespoon olive oil
- salt and freshly ground black pepper
- 2 tablespoons butter
- ¼ cup sour cream
- 3 tablespoons half-and-half (or milk)
- 1¼ cups grated Cheddar cheese, divided
- ¾ teaspoon salt
- freshly ground black pepper
- 1 cup frozen baby broccoli florets, thawed and drained

Directions:

1. Preheat the air fryer to 200°C/400°F.
2. Rub the potatoes all over with olive oil and season generously with salt and freshly ground black pepper. Transfer the potatoes into the air fryer basket and air-fry for 30 minutes, turning the potatoes over halfway through the cooking process.
3. Remove the potatoes from the air fryer and let them rest for 5 minutes. Cut a large oval out of the top of both potatoes. Leaving 1.25 cm of potato flesh around the edge of the potato, scoop the inside of the potato out and into a large bowl to prepare the potato filling. Mash the scooped potato filling with a fork and add the butter, sour cream, half-and-half, 120 grams of the grated Cheddar cheese, salt and pepper to taste. Mix well and then fold in the broccoli florets.
4. Stuff the hollowed out potato shells with the potato and broccoli mixture. Mound the filling high in the potatoes – you will have more filling than room in the potato shells.
5. Transfer the stuffed potatoes back to the air fryer basket and air-fry at 180°C/360°F for 10 minutes. Sprinkle the remaining Cheddar cheese on top of each stuffed potato, lower the heat to 165°C/330°F and air-fry for an additional minute or two to melt cheese.

Variations & Ingredients Tips:

- Add chopped bacon, ham, or prosciutto to the potato filling for a meaty flavor.
- Substitute broccoli with cauliflower, spinach, or kale for different veggie options.
- Top with chopped chives, scallions, or parsley for a fresh garnish.

Per Serving (1 stuffed potato): Calories: 630; Cholesterol: 85mg; Total Fat: 41g; Saturated Fat: 22g; Sodium: 1470mg; Total Carbohydrates: 49g; Dietary Fiber: 5g; Total Sugars: 3g; Protein: 22g

Basic Fried Tofu

Servings: 4 | Prep Time: 10 Minutes (plus 1 Hour Marinating Time) | Cooking Time: 17 Minutes

Ingredients:

- 400 grams extra-firm tofu, drained and pressed
- 1 tablespoon sesame oil
- 2 tablespoons low-sodium soy sauce
- ¼ cup rice vinegar
- 1 tablespoon fresh grated ginger
- 1 clove garlic, minced
- 3 tablespoons cornstarch
- ¼ teaspoon black pepper
- ⅛ teaspoon salt

Directions:

1. Cut the tofu into 16 cubes. Set aside in a glass container with a lid.
2. In a medium bowl, mix the sesame oil, soy sauce, rice vinegar, ginger, and garlic. Pour over the tofu and secure the lid. Place in the refrigerator to marinate for an hour.
3. Preheat the air fryer to 175°C/350°F.
4. In a small bowl, mix the cornstarch, black pepper, and salt.
5. Transfer the tofu to a large bowl and discard the leftover marinade. Pour the cornstarch mixture over the tofu and toss until all the pieces are coated.
6. Liberally spray the air fryer basket with olive oil mist and set the tofu pieces inside. Allow space between the tofu so it can cook evenly. Cook in batches if necessary.

7. Cook 15 to 17 minutes, shaking the basket every 5 minutes to allow the tofu to cook evenly on all sides. When it's done cooking, the tofu will be crisped and browned on all sides.
8. Remove the tofu from the air fryer basket and serve warm.

Variations & Ingredients Tips:

- Add a dash of sriracha or red pepper flakes to the marinade for a spicy kick.
- Serve the fried tofu with a dipping sauce like sweet chili sauce or peanut sauce.
- Use the fried tofu in stir-fries, salads, or rice bowls for a protein-packed meal.

Per Serving: Calories: 180; Cholesterol: 0mg; Total Fat: 11g; Saturated Fat: 1g; Sodium: 370mg; Total Carbohydrates: 10g; Dietary Fiber: 1g; Total Sugars: 1g; Protein: 11g

Pizza Eggplant Rounds

Servings: 4 | Prep Time: 15 Minutes | Cooking Time: 25 Minutes

Ingredients:

- 3 tsp olive oil
- ¼ cup diced onion
- ½ tsp garlic powder
- ½ tsp dried oregano
- ½ cup diced mushrooms
- ½ cup marinara sauce
- 1 eggplant, sliced
- 1 tsp salt
- 1 cup shredded mozzarella
- 2 tbsp Parmesan cheese
- ¼ cup chopped basil

Directions:

1. Warm 2 tsp of olive oil in a skillet over medium heat. Add in onion and mushrooms and cook for 5 minutes until the onions are translucent. Stir in marinara sauce, then add oregano and garlic powder. Turn the heat off.
2. Preheat air fryer at 190°C/375°F.
3. Rub the remaining olive oil over both sides of the eggplant circles. Lay circles on a large plate and sprinkle with salt and black pepper.
4. Top each circle with the marinara sauce mixture and shredded mozzarella and Parmesan cheese.
5. Place eggplant circles in the air fryer basket and Bake for 5 minutes.

6. Scatter with the basil and serve.

Variations & Ingredients Tips:

- Use zucchini or portobello mushroom caps instead of eggplant.
- Add sliced olives, bell peppers, or artichokes for more veggie toppings.
- Drizzle with pesto or balsamic glaze before serving.

Per Serving: Calories: 160; Total Fat: 10g; Saturated Fat: 4g; Sodium: 850mg; Total Carbohydrates: 12g; Dietary Fiber: 4g; Total Sugars: 6g; Protein: 8g

Vegetarian Stuffed Bell Peppers

Servings: 3 | Prep Time: 15 Minutes | Cooking Time: 40 Minutes

Ingredients:

- 1 cup mushrooms, chopped
- 1 tbsp allspice
- 3/4 cup Alfredo sauce
- 1/2 cup canned diced tomatoes
- 1 cup cooked rice
- 2 tbsp dried parsley
- 2 tbsp hot sauce
- Salt and pepper to taste
- 3 large bell peppers

Directions:

1. Preheat air fryer to 190°C/375°F.
2. Whisk mushrooms, allspice and 1 cup of boiling water until smooth.
3. Stir in Alfredo sauce, tomatoes and juices, rice, parsley, hot sauce, salt, and black pepper. Set aside.
4. Cut the top of each bell pepper, take out the core and seeds without breaking the pepper.
5. Fill each pepper with the rice mixture and cover them with a 15-cm square of aluminum foil, folding the edges.
6. Roast for 30 minutes until tender.
7. Let cool completely before unwrapping. Serve immediately.

Variations & Ingredients Tips:

- Use different grains like quinoa or farro instead of rice.
- Add vegan cheese shreds to the filling.

- Top with vegan sour cream or cashew cream.

Per Serving: Calories: 316; Total Fat: 14g; Saturated Fat: 3g; Sodium: 1156mg; Total Carbohydrates: 42g; Dietary Fiber: 5g; Total Sugars: 10g; Protein: 8g

Mexican Twice Air-fried Sweet Potatoes

Servings: 2 | Prep Time: 15 Minutes | Cooking Time: 42 Minutes

Ingredients:

- 2 large sweet potatoes
- Olive oil
- Salt and freshly ground black pepper
- 1/3 cup diced red onion
- 1/3 cup diced red bell pepper
- 1/2 cup canned black beans, drained and rinsed
- 1/2 cup corn kernels, fresh or frozen
- 1/2 teaspoon chili powder
- 1 1/2 cups grated pepper jack cheese, divided
- Jalapeño peppers, sliced

Directions:

1. Preheat the air fryer to 200°C/400°F.
2. Rub the sweet potatoes with olive oil and season with salt and pepper. Air fry at 400°F for 30 minutes, rotating occasionally.
3. Make the filling: Sauté onion and pepper. Add black beans, corn, and chili powder and sauté for 3 minutes. Set aside.
4. Remove potatoes, let rest 5 minutes. Slice off one cm of the flattest sides.
5. Scoop out potato flesh into a bowl, leaving 1.3-cm around edges.
6. Mash potato flesh. Add filling and 1 cup cheese. Season and mix well.
7. Stuff potato shells with filling, mounding high.
8. Air fry stuffed potatoes at 190°C/370°F for 10 minutes.
9. Top with remaining cheese, lower heat to 170°C/340°F and cook 2 more minutes to melt cheese.
10. Top with jalapeños and serve warm.

Variations & Ingredients Tips:

- Use vegan cheese shreds for a dairy-free option.
- Add diced avocado or pico de gallo as toppers.
- Swap black beans for pinto or kidney beans.

Per Serving: Calories: 653; Total Fat: 27g; Saturated Fat: 14g; Sodium: 877mg; Total Carbohydrates: 82g; Dietary Fiber: 16g; Total Sugars: 15g; Protein: 25g

Cheddar-bean Flautas

Servings: 4 | Prep Time: 10 Minutes | Cooking Time: 15 Minutes

Ingredients:

- 8 corn tortillas
- 1 can refried beans
- 1 cup shredded cheddar
- 1 cup guacamole

Directions:

1. Preheat air fryer to 200°C/390°F. Wet the tortillas with water. Spray the frying basket with oil and stack the tortillas inside. Air Fry for 1 minute. Remove to a flat surface, laying them out individually. Scoop an equal amount of beans in a line down the center of each tortilla. Top with cheddar cheese. Roll the tortilla sides over the filling and put seam-side down in the greased frying basket. Air Fry for 7 minutes or until the tortillas are golden and crispy. Serve immediately topped with guacamole.

Variations & Ingredients Tips:

- Use black beans or pinto beans instead of refried beans for a different flavor.
- Add diced onions, jalapeños, or cilantro to the bean mixture for extra kick.
- Serve with salsa, sour cream, or hot sauce on the side.

Per Serving (2 flautas): Calories: 430; Cholesterol: 25mg; Total Fat: 23g; Saturated Fat: 9g; Sodium: 850mg; Total Carbohydrates: 46g; Dietary Fiber: 9g; Total Sugars: 2g; Protein: 16g

Hearty Salad

Servings: 2 | Prep Time: 10 Minutes | Cooking Time: 15 Minutes

Ingredients:

- 142 grams cauliflower, cut into florets
- 2 grated carrots
- 1 tbsp olive oil
- 1 tbsp lemon juice

- 2 tbsp raisins
- 2 tbsp roasted pepitas
- 2 tbsp diced red onion
- ¼ cup mayonnaise
- 1/8 tsp black pepper
- 1 tsp cumin
- ½ tsp chia seeds
- ½ tsp sesame seeds

Directions:

1. Preheat air fryer at 180°C/350°F.
2. Combine the cauliflower, cumin, olive oil, black pepper and lemon juice in a bowl, place it in the air fryer basket, and Bake for 5 minutes.
3. Transfer it to a serving dish. Toss in the remaining ingredients.
4. Let chill covered in the fridge until ready to use.
5. Serve sprinkled with sesame and chia seeds.

Variations & Ingredients Tips:

- Roast other vegetables like broccoli, bell peppers, or eggplant alongside the cauliflower.
- Use dried cranberries or chopped dates instead of raisins.
- Add chopped nuts like almonds or walnuts for extra crunch.

Per Serving: Calories: 310; Total Fat: 24g; Saturated Fat: 3.5g; Sodium: 220mg; Total Carbohydrates: 21g; Dietary Fiber: 6g; Total Sugars: 12g; Protein: 5g

Ricotta Veggie Potpie

Servings: 4 | Prep Time: 20 Minutes | Cooking Time: 30 Minutes

Ingredients:

- 1 ¼ cup flour
- ¾ cup ricotta cheese
- 1 tbsp olive oil
- 1 potato, peeled and diced
- ¼ cup diced mushrooms
- ¼ cup diced carrots
- ¼ cup diced celery
- ¼ cup diced yellow onion
- 1 garlic clove, minced
- 1 tbsp unsalted butter
- 1 cup milk
- ½ tsp ground black pepper
- 1 tsp dried thyme
- 2 tbsp dill, chopped

Directions:

1. Preheat air fryer to 180°C/350°F.
2. Combine 1 cup flour and ricotta cheese in a medium bowl and stir until the dough comes together.
3. Heat oil over medium heat in a small skillet. Stir in potato, mushroom, carrots, dill, thyme, celery, onion, and garlic. Cook for 4-5 minutes, often stirring, until the onions are soft and translucent.
4. Add butter and melt, then stir in the rest of the flour. Slowly pour in the milk and keep stirring. Simmer for 5 minutes until the sauce has thickened, then stir in pepper and thyme.
5. Spoon the vegetable mixture into four 180-ml ramekins. Cut the dough into 4 equal sections and work it into rounds that fit over the size of the ramekins. Top the ramekins with the dough, then place the ramekins in the air fryer basket.
6. Bake for 10 minutes until the crust is golden. Serve hot and enjoy.

Variations & Ingredients Tips:

- Use sweet potato instead of regular potato for a sweeter flavor.
- Add frozen peas or corn to the veggie mix.
- Brush the crust with egg wash for a shinier finish.

Per Serving: Calories: 380; Total Fat: 16g; Saturated Fat: 8g; Sodium: 210mg; Total Carbohydrates: 45g; Dietary Fiber: 3g; Total Sugars: 6g; Protein: 15g

Basil Green Beans

Servings: 4 | Prep Time: 5 Minutes | Cooking Time: 15 Minutes

Ingredients:

- 680 grams green beans, trimmed
- 1 tbsp olive oil
- 1 tbsp fresh basil, chopped
- Garlic salt to taste

Directions:

1. Preheat air fryer to 200°C/400°F. Coat the green beans with olive oil in a large bowl. Combine with fresh basil and garlic salt. Put the beans in the frying basket and Air Fry for 7-9 minutes, shaking once until the beans begin to brown. Serve warm and enjoy!

Variations & Ingredients Tips:

- Add sliced almonds or chopped bacon for extra

crunch and flavor.
- ▸ Substitute basil with other fresh herbs like parsley, thyme, or oregano.
- ▸ Drizzle with balsamic vinegar or lemon juice before serving for a tangy twist.

Per Serving: Calories: 70; Cholesterol: 0mg; Total Fat: 4g; Saturated Fat: 0.5g; Sodium: 75mg; Total Carbohydrates: 9g; Dietary Fiber: 4g; Total Sugars: 4g; Protein: 2g

Italian-style Fried Cauliflower

Servings: 4 | Prep Time: 25 Minutes | Cooking Time: 35 Minutes

Ingredients:

- 2 eggs
- 1/3 cup all-purpose flour
- ½ tsp Italian seasoning
- ½ cup bread crumbs
- 1 tsp garlic powder
- 3 tsp grated Parmesan cheese
- Salt and pepper to taste
- 1 head cauliflower, cut into florets
- ½ tsp ground coriander

Directions:

1. Preheat air fryer to 190°C/370°F.
2. Set out 3 small bowls. In the first, mix the flour with Italian seasoning. In the second, beat the eggs. In the third bowl, combine the crumbs, garlic, Parmesan, ground coriander, salt, and pepper.
3. Dip the cauliflower in the flour, then dredge in egg, and finally in the bread crumb mixture.
4. Place a batch of cauliflower in the greased air fryer basket and spray with cooking oil.
5. Bake for 10-12 minutes, shaking once until golden.
6. Serve warm and enjoy!

Variations & Ingredients Tips:

- ▸ Use panko breadcrumbs for an extra crispy texture.
- ▸ Add red pepper flakes or cayenne to the breading for a spicy kick.
- ▸ Serve with marinara sauce or ranch dressing for dipping.

Per Serving: Calories: 170; Total Fat: 5g; Saturated Fat: 1.5g; Sodium: 410mg; Total Carbohydrates: 24g; Dietary Fiber: 5g; Total Sugars: 4g; Protein: 9g

Vegetable Side Dishes Recipes

Herbed Baby Red Potato Hasselback

Servings: 4 | Prep Time: 10 Minutes | Cooking Time: 35 Minutes

Ingredients:

- 6 baby red potatoes, scrubbed
- 3 tsp shredded cheddar cheese
- 1 tbsp olive oil
- 2 tbsp butter, melted
- 1 tbsp chopped thyme
- Salt and pepper to taste
- 3 tsp sour cream
- 1/4 cup chopped parsley

Directions:

1. Preheat air fryer at 180°C/350°F.
2. Make slices in the width of each potato about 6mm apart without cutting through.
3. Rub potato slices with olive oil, both outside and in-between slices.
4. Place potatoes in the frying basket and air fry for 20 minutes, tossing once.
5. Brush with melted butter, and scatter with thyme.
6. Remove them to a large serving dish. Sprinkle with salt, black pepper and top with a dollop of cheddar

cheese, sour cream.

7. Scatter with parsley to serve.

Variations & Ingredients Tips:

▸ Use fresh rosemary or oregano instead of thyme.
▸ Mix cheese into melted butter before brushing on potatoes.
▸ Serve with ranch or blue cheese dressing for dipping.

Per Serving: Calories: 217; Total Fat: 14g; Saturated Fat: 6g; Cholesterol: 23mg; Sodium: 133mg; Total Carbs: 20g; Dietary Fiber: 3g; Total Sugars: 2g; Protein: 4g

Lovely Mac'n'cheese

Servings: 4 | Prep Time: 10 Minutes | Cooking Time: 40 Minutes

Ingredients:

- 2 cups grated American cheese
- 4 cups elbow macaroni
- 3 eggs, beaten
- 1/2 cup sour cream
- 4 tbsp butter
- 1/2 tsp mustard powder
- 1/2 tsp salt
- 1 cup milk

Directions:

1. Preheat air fryer to 180°C/350°F.
2. Bring a pot of salted water to a boil and cook the macaroni following package instructions. Drain.
3. Add 1 1/2 cups cheese and butter to the hot macaroni and stir to melt.
4. Mix the eggs, milk, sour cream, mustard powder, and salt in a bowl and add to the macaroni; mix gently.
5. Spoon mixture into a greased baking dish and transfer to air fryer.
6. Bake for 15 minutes. Sprinkle with remaining 1/2 cup cheese.
7. Cook 5-8 more minutes until top is bubbling and golden.
8. Serve.

Variations & Ingredients Tips:

▸ Add cooked bacon, ham or peas to the macaroni mixture.
▸ Use a blend of cheeses like cheddar and parmesan.
▸ Top with breadcrumb topping before baking.

Per Serving: Calories: 634; Total Fat: 37g; Saturated Fat: 21g; Cholesterol: 199mg; Sodium: 835mg; Total Carbs: 52g; Dietary Fiber: 2g; Total Sugars: 5g; Protein: 24g

Buttery Stuffed Tomatoes

Servings: 6 | Prep Time: 10 Minutes | Cooking Time: 15 Minutes

Ingredients:

- 3 227g round tomatoes
- ½ cup plus 1 tablespoon Plain panko bread crumbs (gluten-free, if a concern)
- 3 tablespoons (about 14g) Finely grated Parmesan cheese
- 3 tablespoons Butter, melted and cooled
- 4 teaspoons Stemmed and chopped fresh parsley leaves
- 1 teaspoon Minced garlic
- ¼ teaspoon Table salt
- Up to ¼ teaspoon Red pepper flakes
- Olive oil spray

Directions:

1. Preheat the air fryer to 190°C/375°F.
2. Cut the tomatoes in half through their "equators" (that is, not through the stem ends). One at a time, gently squeeze the tomato halves over a trash can, using a clean finger to gently force out the seeds and most of the juice inside, working carefully so that the tomato doesn't lose its round shape or get crushed.
3. Stir the bread crumbs, cheese, butter, parsley, garlic, salt, and red pepper flakes in a bowl until the bread crumbs are moistened and the parsley is uniform throughout the mixture. Pile this mixture into the spaces left in the tomato halves. Press gently to compact the filling. Coat the tops of the tomatoes with olive oil spray.
4. Place the tomatoes cut side up in the basket. They may touch each other. Air-fry for 15 minutes, or until the filling is lightly browned and crunchy.
5. Use nonstick-safe spatula and kitchen tongs for balance to gently transfer the stuffed tomatoes to a platter or a cutting board. Cool for a couple of minutes before serving.

Variations & Ingredients Tips:

▸ Add crumbled feta or gorgonzola to the bread crumb mixture.

- Substitute basil or oregano for the parsley.
- Drizzle with balsamic glaze before serving.

Per Serving: Calories: 135; Total Fat: 7g; Saturated Fat: 3g; Cholesterol: 13mg; Sodium: 310mg; Total Carbs: 15g; Fiber: 2g; Sugars: 4g; Protein: 4g

Broccoli Tots

Servings: 24 Tots | Prep Time: 10 Minutes | Cooking Time: 10 Minutes

Ingredients:

- 2 cups (225g) broccoli florets
- 1 egg, beaten
- ⅛ teaspoon onion powder
- ¼ teaspoon salt
- ⅛ teaspoon pepper
- 2 tablespoons grated Parmesan cheese
- ¼ cup panko breadcrumbs
- Oil for misting

Directions:

1. Steam broccoli for 2 minutes. Rinse in cold water, drain well, and chop finely.
2. In a large bowl, mix broccoli with all other ingredients except the oil.
3. Scoop out small portions of mixture and shape into 24 tots. Lay them on a cookie sheet or wax paper as you work.
4. Spray tots with oil and place in air fryer basket in single layer.
5. Cook at 198°C/390°F for 5 minutes. Shake basket and spray with oil again. Cook 5 minutes longer or until browned and crispy.

Variations & Ingredients Tips:

- Substitute cauliflower for the broccoli.
- Add shredded cheddar or feta to the mixture.
- Serve with ranch, marinara or garlic aioli for dipping.

Per Serving: Calories: 30; Total Fat: 1g; Saturated Fat: 0g; Cholesterol: 15mg; Sodium: 85mg; Total Carbs: 4g; Fiber: 1g; Sugars: 0g; Protein: 2g

Chicken Salad With Sunny Citrus Dressing

Servings: 4 | Prep Time: 15 Minutes | Cooking Time: 8 Minutes

Ingredients:

- Sunny Citrus Dressing
- 1 cup first cold-pressed extra virgin olive oil
- ⅓ cup red wine vinegar
- 2 tablespoons all natural orange marmalade
- 1 teaspoon dry mustard
- 1 teaspoon ground black pepper
- California Chicken
- 4 large chicken tenders
- 1 teaspoon olive oil
- Juice of 1 small orange or clementine
- Salt and pepper
- ½ teaspoon rosemary
- Salad
- 8 cups romaine or leaf lettuce, chopped or torn into bite-size pieces
- 2 clementines or small oranges, peeled and sectioned
- ½ cup dried cranberries
- 4 tablespoons sliced almonds

Directions:

1. Make dressing: In a jar, combine all dressing ingredients and shake until blended. Refrigerate 30 mins.
2. Brush tenders with 1 tsp oil. Drizzle orange juice over them and season with salt, pepper, rosemary.
3. Cook at 198°C/390°F for 3 mins, turn over, cook 5 more mins until juices run clear.
4. To serve: Toss lettuce with 2 tbsp dressing. Divide among 4 plates.
5. Top with chicken, clementines, cranberries and almonds. Pass extra dressing.

Variations & Ingredients Tips:

- Use spinach or arugula instead of romaine.
- Add sliced avocado or cucumber.
- Substitute honey mustard or balsamic vinaigrette for dressing.

Per Serving: Calories: 545; Total Fat: 37g; Saturated Fat: 5g; Cholesterol: 50mg; Sodium: 220mg; Total Carbs: 31g; Fiber: 9g; Sugars: 19g; Protein: 27g

Acorn Squash Halves With Maple Butter Glaze

Servings: 2 | Prep Time: 10 Minutes | Cooking Time: 33 Minutes

Ingredients:

- 1 medium (454g to 567g) Acorn squash
- Vegetable oil spray
- ¼ teaspoon Table salt
- 1½ tablespoons Butter, melted
- 1½ tablespoons Maple syrup

Directions:

1. Preheat the air fryer to 162°C/325°F (or 166°C/330°F, if that's the closest setting).
2. Cut a squash in half through the stem end. Use a flatware spoon (preferably, a serrated grapefruit spoon) to scrape out and discard the seeds and membranes in each half. Use a paring knife to make a crisscross pattern of cuts about 1.3 cm apart and 0.6 cm deep across the "meat" of the squash. If working with a second squash, repeat this step for that one.
3. Generously coat the cut side of the squash halves with vegetable oil spray. Sprinkle the halves with the salt. Set them in the basket cut side up with at least 0.6 cm between them. Air-fry undisturbed for 30 minutes.
4. Increase the machine's temperature to 204°C/400°F. Mix the melted butter and syrup in a small bowl until uniform. Brush this mixture over the cut sides of the squash(es), letting it pool in the center. Air-fry undisturbed for 3 minutes, or until the glaze is bubbling.
5. Use a nonstick-safe spatula and kitchen tongs to transfer the squash halves cut side up to a wire rack. Cool for 5 to 10 minutes before serving.

Variations & Ingredients Tips:

- Substitute brown sugar for the maple syrup for a different flavor profile.
- Add chopped pecans or walnuts to the glaze for crunch.
- Sprinkle with cinnamon or pumpkin pie spice before glazing.

Per Serving: Calories: 207; Total Fat: 9g; Saturated Fat: 5g; Cholesterol: 20mg; Sodium: 230mg; Total Carbs: 33g; Fiber: 3g; Sugars: 12g; Protein: 2g

Butternut Medallions With Honey Butter And Sage

Servings: 2 | Prep Time: 10 Minutes | Cooking Time: 15 Minutes

Ingredients:

- 1 butternut squash, peeled
- Olive oil, in a spray bottle
- Salt and freshly ground black pepper
- 2 tablespoons butter, softened
- 2 tablespoons honey
- Pinch ground cinnamon
- Pinch ground nutmeg
- Chopped fresh sage

Directions:

1. Preheat the air fryer to 188°C/370°F.
2. Cut the neck of the butternut squash into disks about 1.3cm thick. (Use the base of the butternut squash for another use.) Brush or spray the disks with oil and season with salt and freshly ground black pepper.
3. Transfer the butternut disks to the air fryer in one layer (or just ever so slightly overlapping). Air-fry at 188°C/370°F for 5 minutes.
4. While the butternut squash is cooking, combine the butter, honey, cinnamon and nutmeg in a small bowl. Brush this mixture on the butternut squash, flip the disks over and brush the other side as well. Continue to air-fry at 188°C/370°F for another 5 minutes. Flip the disks once more, brush with more of the honey butter and air-fry for another 5 minutes. The butternut should be browning nicely around the edges.
5. Remove the butternut squash from the air-fryer and repeat with additional batches if necessary. Transfer to a serving platter, sprinkle with the fresh sage and serve.

Variations & Ingredients Tips:

- Substitute brown sugar for the honey.
- Add a sprinkle of cayenne pepper or chili powder for a kick.
- Toss with chopped pecans or walnuts before serving.

Per Serving: Calories: 290; Total Fat: 13g; Saturated Fat: 7g; Cholesterol: 30mg; Sodium: 140mg; Total Carbs: 43g; Fiber: 5g; Sugars: 16g; Protein: 2g

Steamboat Shrimp Salad

Servings: 4 | Prep Time: 10 Minutes | Cooking Time: 4 Minutes

Ingredients:

- Steamboat Dressing
- ½ cup mayonnaise
- ½ cup plain yogurt
- 2 teaspoons freshly squeezed lemon juice (no substitutes)

- 2 teaspoons grated lemon rind
- 1 teaspoon dill weed, slightly crushed
- ½ teaspoon hot sauce
- Steamed Shrimp
- 24 small, raw shrimp, peeled and deveined
- 1 teaspoon lemon juice
- ¼ teaspoon Old Bay Seasoning
- Salad
- 8 cups romaine or Bibb lettuce, chopped or torn
- ¼ cup red onion, cut in thin slivers
- 12 black olives, sliced
- 12 cherry or grape tomatoes, halved
- 1 medium avocado, sliced or cut into large chunks

Directions:

1. Combine all dressing ingredients and mix well. Refrigerate while preparing shrimp and salad.
2. Sprinkle raw shrimp with lemon juice and Old Bay Seasoning. Use more Old Bay if you like your shrimp bold and spicy.
3. Pour 4 tablespoons of water in bottom of air fryer.
4. Place shrimp in air fryer basket in single layer.
5. Cook at 200°C/390°F for 4 minutes. Remove shrimp from basket and place in refrigerator to cool.
6. Combine all salad ingredients and mix gently. Divide among 4 salad plates or bowls.
7. Top each salad with 6 shrimp and serve with dressing.

Variations & Ingredients Tips:

- Use different types of lettuce, such as spinach or arugula, for a different flavor and texture.
- Add some crumbled bacon or sliced hard-boiled eggs for extra protein.
- For a vegan version, replace the shrimp with roasted chickpeas or tofu and use a vegan mayonnaise in the dressing.

Per Serving: Calories: 390; Total Fat: 32g; Saturated Fat: 5g; Cholesterol: 135mg; Sodium: 670mg; Total Carbs: 12g; Fiber: 6g; Sugars: 4g; Protein: 18g

Pork Tenderloin Salad

Servings: 4 | Prep Time: 15 Minutes | Cooking Time: 25 Minutes

Ingredients:

- Pork Tenderloin:
- 1/2 teaspoon smoked paprika
- 1/4 teaspoon salt
- 1/4 teaspoon garlic powder
- 1/2 teaspoon onion powder
- 1/8 teaspoon ginger
- 1 teaspoon extra-light olive oil
- 340g pork tenderloin
- Dressing:
- 3 tablespoons extra-light olive oil
- 2 tablespoons red wine vinegar
- 2 tablespoons Dijon mustard
- 1 tablespoon honey
- Salad:
- 1/4 sweet red bell pepper
- 1 large Granny Smith apple
- 8 cups shredded napa cabbage

Directions:

1. Mix tenderloin seasonings with oil and rub over pork.
2. Place tenderloin in air fryer basket and cook at 199°C/390°F for 25 mins until 54°C/130°F internal temp.
3. Let meat rest while preparing salad and dressing.
4. Make dressing by shaking all ingredients in a jar until mixed.
5. Cut bell pepper into strips, core and slice apple.
6. Toss cabbage, pepper, apple and dressing in a bowl.
7. Divide salad among plates and top with sliced pork tenderloin.
8. Serve with veggie chips.

Variations & Ingredients Tips:

- Use chicken breast or beef tenderloin instead of pork.
- Add crumbled feta, walnuts or dried cranberries to the salad.
- Serve the tenderloin over mashed potatoes or rice instead.

Per Serving: 310 Calories; 14g Total Fat; 3g Saturated Fat; 63mg Cholesterol; 403mg Sodium; 26g Total Carbs; 5g Fiber; 16g Sugars; 21g Protein

Honey-mustard Asparagus Puffs

Servings: 4 | Prep Time: 10 Minutes | Cooking Time: 35 Minutes

Ingredients:

- 8 asparagus spears

- 1/2 sheet puff pastry
- 2 tbsp honey mustard
- 1 egg, lightly beaten

Directions:

1. Preheat the air fryer to 190°C/375°F.
2. Spread the pastry with honey mustard and cut it into 8 strips.
3. Wrap the pastry, honey mustard-side in, around the asparagus.
4. Put a rack in the frying basket and lay the asparagus spears on the rack.
5. Brush all over pastries with beaten egg and air fry for 12-17 minutes or until the pastry is golden.
6. Serve.

Variations & Ingredients Tips:

- Use puff pastry sheets instead of sheets for easier wrapping.
- Brush with an egg wash before cooking for a shiny finish.
- Sprinkle with parmesan cheese before baking.

Per Serving: Calories: 148; Total Fat: 9g; Saturated Fat: 3g; Cholesterol: 77mg; Sodium: 321mg; Total Carbs: 14g; Dietary Fiber: 1g; Total Sugars: 5g; Protein: 4g

Simple Roasted Sweet Potatoes

Servings: 2 | Prep Time: 5 Minutes | Cooking Time: 45 Minutes

Ingredients:

- 2 sweet potatoes (280 to 340 g each)

Directions:

1. Preheat the air fryer to 180°C/350°F.
2. Prick the sweet potato(es) in four or five different places with the tines of a flatware fork (not in a line but all around).
3. When the machine is at temperature, set the sweet potato(es) in the basket with as much air space between them as possible. Air-fry undisturbed for 45 minutes, or until soft when pricked with a fork.
4. Use kitchen tongs to transfer the sweet potato(es) to a wire rack. Cool for 5 minutes before serving.

Variations & Ingredients Tips:

- Serve the sweet potatoes with butter, cinnamon, or brown sugar for a sweeter flavor.
- Cut the sweet potatoes into wedges or fries for a different shape and texture.
- Try using different types of sweet potatoes, such as purple or Japanese sweet potatoes, for a unique color and flavor.

Per Serving: Calories: 180; Total Fat: 0g; Saturated Fat: 0g; Cholesterol: 0mg; Sodium: 70mg; Total Carbs: 41g; Fiber: 6g; Sugars: 13g; Protein: 4g

Pecorino Dill Muffins

Servings: 4 | Prep Time: 10 Minutes | Cooking Time: 25 Minutes

Ingredients:

- 1/4 cup grated Pecorino cheese
- 1 cup flour
- 1 tsp dried dill
- 1/8 tsp salt
- 1/4 tsp onion powder
- 2 tsp baking powder
- 1 egg
- 1/4 cup Greek yogurt

Directions:

1. Preheat air fryer to 180°C/350°F.
2. In a bowl, combine the dry ingredients (pecorino, flour, dill, salt, onion powder, baking powder).
3. In another bowl, whisk the wet ingredients (egg, yogurt).
4. Add wet to dry ingredients and stir until just combined.
5. Transfer batter to 6 greased silicone muffin cups.
6. Place muffin cups in air fryer basket and bake for 12 minutes.
7. Serve right away.

Variations & Ingredients Tips:

- Use cheddar or parmesan cheese instead of pecorino.
- Add chopped chives or green onions to the batter.
- Substitute milk or buttermilk for the Greek yogurt.

Per Serving: Calories: 153; Total Fat: 5g; Saturated Fat: 2g; Cholesterol: 36mg; Sodium: 301mg; Total Carbohydrates: 21g; Dietary Fiber: 1g; Total Sugars: 2g; Protein: 7g

Florentine Stuffed Tomatoes

Servings: 2 | Prep Time: 10 Minutes | Cooking Time: 12 Minutes

Ingredients:

- 1 cup frozen spinach, thawed and squeezed dry
- ¼ cup toasted pine nuts
- ¼ cup grated mozzarella cheese
- ½ cup crumbled feta cheese
- ½ cup coarse fresh breadcrumbs
- 1 tablespoon olive oil
- Salt and freshly ground black pepper
- 2 to 3 beefsteak tomatoes, halved horizontally and insides scooped out

Directions:

1. Combine spinach, pine nuts, mozzarella, feta, breadcrumbs, olive oil, salt and pepper in a bowl.
2. Spoon the mixture into the tomato halves, enough for 2-3 tomatoes.
3. Preheat air fryer to 177°C/350°F.
4. Place 3-4 stuffed tomato halves in the air fryer basket and cook for 12 mins until tops are lightly browned.
5. Let cool 1-2 mins before serving.

Variations & Ingredients Tips:

- Use panko breadcrumbs instead of fresh.
- Substitute parmesan for the feta cheese.
- Add minced garlic or lemon zest to the filling.

Per Serving: Calories: 390; Total Fat: 24g; Saturated Fat: 7g; Cholesterol: 35mg; Sodium: 790mg; Total Carbs: 32g; Fiber: 6g; Sugars: 9g; Protein: 17g

Grits Again

Servings: 2 | Prep Time: 15 Minutes | Cooking Time: 10 Minutes

Ingredients:

- Cooked grits
- Plain breadcrumbs
- Oil for misting or cooking spray
- Honey or maple syrup for serving (optional)

Directions:

1. While grits are still warm, spread them into a square or rectangular baking pan, about 1-2 cm thick.
2. Chill several hours or overnight, until grits are cold and firm.
3. When ready to cook, pour off any water that has collected in pan and cut grits into 5-8 cm squares.
4. Dip grits squares in breadcrumbs and place in air fryer basket in single layer, close but not touching.
5. Cook at 199°C/390°F for 10 minutes, until heated through and crispy brown on the outside.
6. Serve while hot either plain or with a drizzle of honey or maple syrup.

Variations & Ingredients Tips:

- Mix cheese like cheddar into the grits before chilling.
- Dip in beaten egg before breading for an extra crispy crust.
- Season the breadcrumbs with herbs and spices.

Per Serving: Calories: 230; Total Fat: 3g; Saturated Fat: 0g; Cholesterol: 0mg; Sodium: 280mg; Total Carbohydrates: 45g; Dietary Fiber: 2g; Total Sugars: 1g; Protein: 5g

Truffle Vegetable Croquettes

Servings: 4 | Prep Time: 20 Minutes | Cooking Time: 40 Minutes

Ingredients:

- 2 cooked potatoes, mashed
- 1 cooked carrot, mashed
- 1 tablespoon onion, minced
- 2 eggs, beaten
- 2 tablespoons melted butter
- 1 tablespoon truffle oil
- ½ tablespoon flour
- Salt and pepper to taste

Directions:

1. Preheat air fryer to 180°C/350°F.
2. Sift the flour, salt, and pepper in a bowl and stir to combine.
3. Add the potatoes, carrot, onion, butter, and truffle oil to a separate bowl and mix well.
4. Shape the potato mixture into small bite-sized patties.
5. Dip the potato patties into the beaten eggs, coating thoroughly, then roll in the flour mixture to cover all sides.
6. Arrange the croquettes in the greased frying basket and Air Fry for 14-16 minutes. Halfway through cook-

ing, shake the basket. The croquettes should be crispy and golden.
7. Serve hot and enjoy!

Variations & Ingredients Tips:

▶ Use different types of vegetables, such as sweet potatoes or parsnips, for a variety of flavors and textures.
▶ Add some grated Parmesan cheese or nutritional yeast to the potato mixture for a cheesy flavor.
▶ Serve the croquettes with a dipping sauce, such as garlic aioli or tomato sauce.

Per Serving: Calories: 220; Total Fat: 16g; Saturated Fat: 6g; Cholesterol: 110mg; Sodium: 120mg; Total Carbs: 15g; Fiber: 2g; Sugars: 2g; Protein: 5g

French Fries

Servings: 4 | Prep Time: 10 Minutes | Cooking Time: 25 Minutes

Ingredients:

- 2 cups fresh potatoes
- 2 teaspoons oil
- ½ teaspoon salt

Directions:

1. Cut potatoes into 3cm-wide slices, then into 1.3cm sticks.
2. Rinse potato sticks and blot dry.
3. In a bowl, mix the potatoes, oil, and salt.
4. Pour into air fryer basket.
5. Cook at 198°C/390°F for 10 mins. Shake basket and cook 15 more mins until golden brown.

Variations & Ingredients Tips:

▶ Toss with cajun seasoning or ranch before cooking.
▶ Use sweet potato fries instead of russet.
▶ Drizzle with truffle oil and parmesan after frying.

Per Serving: Calories: 120; Total Fat: 3g; Saturated Fat: 0g; Cholesterol: 0mg; Sodium: 200mg; Total Carbs: 22g; Fiber: 2g; Sugars: 1g; Protein: 2g

Stunning Apples & Onions

Servings: 4 | Prep Time: 5 Minutes | Cooking Time: 30 Minutes

Ingredients:

- 2 peeled McIntosh apples, sliced
- 1 shallot, sliced
- 2 teaspoons canola oil
- 2 tablespoons brown sugar
- 1 tablespoon honey
- 1 tablespoon butter, melted
- ½ teaspoon sea salt

Directions:

1. Preheat the air fryer to 165°C/325°F.
2. Toss the shallot slices with oil in a bowl until coated. Put the bowl in the fryer and Bake for 5 minutes.
3. Remove the bowl and add the apples, brown sugar, honey, melted butter, and sea salt and stir.
4. Put the bowl back into the fryer and Bake for 10-12 more minutes or until the onions and apples are tender.
5. Stir again and serve.

Variations & Ingredients Tips:

▶ Use different types of apples, such as Granny Smith or Honeycrisp, for a variety of flavors and textures.
▶ Add some chopped nuts, such as pecans or walnuts, for a crunchy texture.
▶ For a savory version, replace the brown sugar and honey with balsamic vinegar and thyme.

Per Serving: Calories: 140; Total Fat: 5g; Saturated Fat: 2g; Cholesterol: 10mg; Sodium: 300mg; Total Carbs: 25g; Fiber: 2g; Sugars: 20g; Protein: 0g

Perfect Broccoli

Servings: 4 | Prep Time: 5 Minutes | Cooking Time: 12 Minutes

Ingredients:

- 5 cups (624g) fresh broccoli florets
- Olive oil spray
- 3/4 teaspoon table salt

Directions:

1. Preheat air fryer to 190°C/375°F.
2. Place broccoli florets in a bowl and coat generously with olive oil spray, tossing to evenly coat.
3. Sprinkle with salt and toss again.
4. Pour florets into air fryer basket in an even layer.
5. Air fry for 10 minutes, tossing and rearranging pieces twice during cooking until lightly browned but still crunchy.

6. Transfer florets to a serving bowl and let cool 1-2 minutes before serving hot.

Variations & Ingredients Tips:

- Add minced garlic or red pepper flakes before cooking.
- Toss with lemon juice, parmesan or breadcrumbs after cooking.
- Use frozen broccoli florets and increase cook time by 2-3 minutes.

Per Serving: Calories: 33; Total Fat: 1g; Saturated Fat: 0g; Cholesterol: 0mg; Sodium: 298mg; Total Carbohydrates: 5g; Dietary Fiber: 3g; Total Sugars: 2g; Protein: 3g

Grits Casserole

Servings: 4 | Prep Time: 10 Minutes | Cooking Time: 30 Minutes

Ingredients:

- 10 fresh asparagus spears, cut into 2.5-cm pieces
- 2 cups cooked grits, cooled to room temperature
- 1 egg, beaten
- 2 teaspoons Worcestershire sauce
- 1/2 teaspoon garlic powder
- 1/4 teaspoon salt
- 2 slices provolone cheese (about 1 15-g)
- Oil for misting or cooking spray

Directions:

1. Mist asparagus spears with oil and cook at 200°C/390°F for 5 minutes, until crisp-tender.
2. In a medium bowl, mix together the grits, egg, Worcestershire, garlic powder, and salt.
3. Spoon half of grits mixture into air fryer baking pan and top with asparagus.
4. Tear cheese slices into pieces and layer evenly on top of asparagus.
5. Top with remaining grits.
6. Bake at 180°C/360°F for 25 minutes. The casserole will rise a little as it cooks. When done, the top will have browned lightly with just a hint of crispiness.

Variations & Ingredients Tips:

- Substitute broccoli, spinach or mushrooms for the asparagus.
- Use different cheese varieties like cheddar or pepper jack.
- Add crumbled bacon or ham to the grits mixture.

Per Serving: Calories: 210; Total Fat: 8g; Saturated Fat: 4g; Cholesterol: 65mg; Sodium: 420mg; Total Carbohydrates: 26g; Dietary Fiber: 1g; Total Sugars: 1g; Protein: 9g

Roasted Corn Salad

Servings: 3 | Prep Time: 10 Minutes | Cooking Time: 15 Minutes

Ingredients:

- 3 (10cm) lengths husked and de-silked corn on the cob
- Olive oil spray
- 1 cup packed baby arugula leaves
- 12 cherry tomatoes, halved
- Up to 3 medium scallions, trimmed and thinly sliced
- 2 tablespoons lemon juice
- 1 tablespoon olive oil
- 1 1/2 teaspoons honey
- 1/4 teaspoon mild paprika
- 1/4 teaspoon dried oregano
- 1/4 teaspoon + more to taste table salt
- 1/4 teaspoon ground black pepper

Directions:

1. Preheat air fryer to 205°C/400°F.
2. Coat corn cobs lightly with olive oil spray. Place in air fryer basket, spaced apart. Air fry 15 minutes until charred in spots.
3. Let corn cool 15 minutes. Cut kernels off the cobs.
4. In a bowl, combine corn kernels, chopped arugula, tomatoes and scallions.
5. Make dressing by whisking lemon juice, olive oil, honey, paprika, oregano, salt and pepper.
6. Pour dressing over salad and toss to coat. Season with more salt if needed.

Variations & Ingredients Tips:

- Use grilled corn if not in season.
- Add crumbled feta or diced avocado.
- Substitute lime juice for the lemon juice in the dressing.

Per Serving: Calories: 152; Total Fat: 6g; Saturated Fat: 1g; Cholesterol: 0mg; Sodium: 119mg; Total Carbohydrates: 24g; Dietary Fiber: 4g; Total Sugars: 9g; Protein: 4g

Buttered Brussels Sprouts

Servings: 4 | Prep Time: 5 Minutes | Cooking Time: 30 Minutes

Ingredients:

- ¼ cup grated Parmesan
- 2 tbsp butter, melted
- 455g Brussels sprouts
- Salt and pepper to taste

Directions:

1. Preheat air fryer to 165°C/330°F.
2. Trim the bottoms of the sprouts and remove any discolored leaves.
3. Place the sprouts in a medium bowl along with butter, salt and pepper. Toss to coat, then place them in the frying basket.
4. Roast for 20 minutes, shaking the basket twice. When done, the sprouts should be crisp with golden-brown color.
5. Plate the sprouts in a serving dish and toss with Parmesan cheese.

Variations & Ingredients Tips:

- Add crushed garlic or garlic powder to the butter mixture.
- Toss with balsamic glaze or lemon juice after cooking.
- Use olive oil instead of butter to make it vegan.

Per Serving: Calories: 130; Total Fat: 8g; Saturated Fat: 4g; Cholesterol: 15mg; Sodium: 230mg; Total Carbs: 11g; Fiber: 4g; Sugars: 3g; Protein: 6g

Sandwiches And Burgers Recipes

Reuben Sandwiches

Servings: 2 | Prep Time: 10 Minutes | Cooking Time: 11 Minutes

Ingredients:

- 225 grams Sliced deli corned beef
- 4 teaspoons Regular or low-fat mayonnaise (not fat-free)
- 4 Rye bread slices
- 2 tablespoons plus 2 teaspoons Russian dressing
- ½ cup Purchased sauerkraut, squeezed by the handful over the sink to get rid of excess moisture
- 55 grams (2 to 4 slices) Swiss cheese slices (optional)

Directions:

1. Set the corned beef in the basket, slip the basket into the machine, and heat the air fryer to 200°C/400°F. Air-fry undisturbed for 3 minutes from the time the basket is put in the machine, just to warm up the meat.
2. Use kitchen tongs to transfer the corned beef to a cutting board. Spread 1 teaspoon mayonnaise on one side of each slice of rye bread, rubbing the mayonnaise into the bread with a small flatware knife.
3. Place the bread slices mayonnaise side down on a cutting board. Spread the Russian dressing over the "dry" side of each slice. For one sandwich, top one slice of bread with the corned beef, sauerkraut, and cheese (if using). For two sandwiches, top two slices of bread each with half of the corned beef, sauerkraut, and cheese (if using). Close the sandwiches with the remaining bread, setting it mayonnaise side up on top.
4. Set the sandwich(es) in the basket and air-fry undisturbed for 8 minutes, or until browned and crunchy.
5. Use a nonstick-safe spatula, and perhaps a flatware fork for balance, to transfer the sandwich(es) to a cutting board. Cool for 2 or 3 minutes before slicing in half and serving.

Variations & Ingredients Tips:

- Substitute corned beef with pastrami for a classic New York deli taste.
- Use Thousand Island dressing instead of Russian dressing for a tangy, sweet flavor.
- Add sliced dill pickles or mustard to the sandwich for extra zing.

Per Serving (1 sandwich): Calories: 520; Cholesterol: 75mg; Total Fat: 30g; Saturated Fat: 9g; Sodium: 2020mg; Total Carbohydrates: 36g; Dietary Fiber: 4g; Total Sugars: 6g; Protein: 29g

Thai-style Pork Sliders

Servings: 4 | Prep Time: 15 Minutes | Cooking Time: 15 Minutes

Ingredients:

- 310 grams Ground pork
- 2½ tablespoons Very thinly sliced scallions, white and green parts
- 4 teaspoons Minced peeled fresh ginger
- 2½ teaspoons Fish sauce (gluten-free, if a concern)
- 2 teaspoons Thai curry paste (see the headnote; gluten-free, if a concern)
- 2 teaspoons Light brown sugar
- ¾ teaspoon Ground black pepper
- 4 Slider buns (gluten-free, if a concern)

Directions:

1. Preheat the air fryer to 190°C/375°F.
2. Gently mix the pork, scallions, ginger, fish sauce, curry paste, brown sugar, and black pepper in a bowl until well combined. With clean, wet hands, form about 80 grams of the pork mixture into a slider about 6.5-cm in diameter. Repeat until you use up all the meat—3 sliders for the small batch, 4 for the medium, and 6 for the large. (Keep wetting your hands to help the patties adhere.)
3. When the machine is at temperature, set the sliders in the basket in one layer. Air-fry undisturbed for 14 minutes, or until the sliders are golden brown and caramelized at their edges and an instant-read meat thermometer inserted into the center of a slider registers 70°C/160°F.
4. Use a nonstick-safe spatula, and perhaps a flatware fork for balance, to transfer the sliders to a cutting board. Set the buns cut side down in the basket in one layer (working in batches as necessary) and air-fry undisturbed for 1 minute, to toast a bit and warm up. Serve the sliders warm in the buns.

Variations & Ingredients Tips:

- Use ground chicken or turkey for a leaner slider option.
- Substitute Thai curry paste with red curry paste or green curry paste for a different flavor profile.
- Serve with pickled vegetables, cilantro, and sriracha mayonnaise for extra Thai-inspired toppings.

Per Serving (1 slider): Calories: 240; Cholesterol: 65mg; Total Fat: 13g; Saturated Fat: 4g; Sodium: 490mg; Total Carbohydrates: 18g; Dietary Fiber: 1g; Total Sugars: 4g; Protein: 15g

Best-ever Roast Beef Sandwiches

Servings: 6 | Prep Time: 10 Minutes | Cooking Time: 30-50 Minutes

Ingredients:

- 2½ teaspoons Olive oil
- 1½ teaspoons Dried oregano
- 1½ teaspoons Dried thyme
- 1½ teaspoons Onion powder
- 1½ teaspoons Table salt
- 1½ teaspoons Ground black pepper
- 1 kg Beef eye of round
- 6 Round soft rolls, such as Kaiser rolls or hamburger buns (gluten-free, if a concern), split open lengthwise
- ¾ cup Regular, low-fat, or fat-free mayonnaise (gluten-free, if a concern)
- 6 Romaine lettuce leaves, rinsed
- 6 Round tomato slices (0.5 cm thick)

Directions:

1. Preheat the air fryer to 180°C/350°F.
2. Mix the oil, oregano, thyme, onion powder, salt, and pepper in a small bowl. Spread this mixture all over the eye of round.
3. When the machine is at temperature, set the beef in the basket and air-fry for 30 to 50 minutes (the range depends on the size of the cut), turning the meat twice, until an instant-read meat thermometer inserted into the thickest piece of the meat registers 55°C/130°F for rare, 60°C/140°F for medium, or 65°C/150°F for well-done.
4. Use kitchen tongs to transfer the beef to a cutting board. Cool for 10 minutes. If serving now, carve into

3-mm-thick slices. Spread each roll with 2 tablespoons mayonnaise and divide the beef slices between the rolls. Top with a lettuce leaf and a tomato slice and serve. Or set the beef in a container, cover, and refrigerate for up to 3 days to make cold roast beef sandwiches anytime.

Variations & Ingredients Tips:

- Experiment with different herbs and spices in the rub, such as garlic powder, paprika, or rosemary.
- Add sliced red onions or pickles for extra flavor and crunch.
- Use leftover roast beef for cold sandwiches or salads.

Per Serving: Calories: 560; Cholesterol: 115mg; Total Fat: 27g; Saturated Fat: 6g; Sodium: 980mg; Total Carbohydrates: 32g; Dietary Fiber: 2g; Total Sugars: 4g; Protein: 47g

Eggplant Parmesan Subs

Servings: 2 | Prep Time: 10 Minutes | Cooking Time: 13 Minutes

Ingredients:

- 4 Peeled eggplant slices (about 1.25 cm thick and 7.5 cm in diameter)
- Olive oil spray
- 2 tablespoons plus 2 teaspoons Jarred pizza sauce, any variety except creamy
- ¼ cup (about 20 grams) Finely grated Parmesan cheese
- 2 Small, long soft rolls, such as hero, hoagie, or Italian sub rolls (gluten-free, if a concern), split open lengthwise

Directions:

1. Preheat the air fryer to 175°C/350°F.
2. When the machine is at temperature, coat both sides of the eggplant slices with olive oil spray. Set them in the basket in one layer and air-fry undisturbed for 10 minutes, until lightly browned and softened.
3. Increase the machine's temperature to 190°C/375°F (or 185°C/370°F, if that's the closest setting—unless the machine is already at 180°C/360°F, in which case leave it alone). Top each eggplant slice with 2 teaspoons pizza sauce, then 1 tablespoon of cheese. Air-fry undisturbed for 2 minutes, or until the cheese has melted.
4. Use a nonstick-safe spatula, and perhaps a flatware fork for balance, to transfer the eggplant slices cheese side up to a cutting board. Set the roll(s) cut side down in the basket in one layer (working in batches as necessary) and air-fry undisturbed for 1 minute, to toast the rolls a bit and warm them up. Set 2 eggplant slices in each warm roll.

Variations & Ingredients Tips:

- Use zucchini slices instead of eggplant for a different vegetable option.
- Add a slice of fresh mozzarella on top of the Parmesan for extra cheesiness.
- Sprinkle some dried herbs like oregano or basil on the eggplant before cooking for extra flavor.

Per Serving (1 sandwich): Calories: 280; Cholesterol: 10mg; Total Fat: 9g; Saturated Fat: 3g; Sodium: 840mg; Total Carbohydrates: 40g; Dietary Fiber: 5g; Total Sugars: 8g; Protein: 11g

Mexican Cheeseburgers

Servings: 4 | Prep Time: 20 Minutes | Cooking Time: 22 Minutes

Ingredients:

- 570 grams ground beef
- ¼ cup finely chopped onion
- ½ cup crushed yellow corn tortilla chips
- 1 (35-gram) packet taco seasoning
- ¼ cup canned diced green chilies
- 1 egg, lightly beaten
- 115 grams pepper jack cheese, grated
- 4 (30-cm) flour tortillas
- shredded lettuce, sour cream, guacamole, salsa (for topping)

Directions:

1. Combine the ground beef, minced onion, crushed tortilla chips, taco seasoning, green chilies, and egg in a large bowl. Mix thoroughly until combined – your hands are good tools for this. Divide the meat into four equal portions and shape each portion into an oval-shaped burger.
2. Preheat the air fryer to 190°C/370°F.
3. Air-fry the burgers for 18 minutes, turning them over halfway through the cooking time. Divide the cheese between the burgers, lower fryer to 170°C/340°F and air-fry for an additional 4 minutes to melt the cheese. (This will give you a burger that is medium-well. If you prefer your cheeseburger medium-rare, shorten the

cooking time to about 15 minutes and then add the cheese and proceed with the recipe.)
4. While the burgers are cooking, warm the tortillas wrapped in aluminum foil in a 175°C/350°F oven, or in a skillet with a little oil over medium-high heat for a couple of minutes. Keep the tortillas warm until the burgers are ready.
5. To assemble the burgers, spread sour cream over three quarters of the tortillas and top each with some shredded lettuce and salsa. Place the Mexican cheeseburgers on the lettuce and top with guacamole. Fold the tortillas around the burger, starting with the bottom and then folding the sides in over the top. (A little sour cream can help hold the seam of the tortilla together.) Serve immediately.

Variations & Ingredients Tips:

- Use ground turkey or chicken for a leaner burger option.
- Substitute pepper jack cheese with Monterey Jack or cheddar cheese if preferred.
- Add sliced jalapeños or hot sauce to the burger mixture for extra heat.

Per Serving (1 burger): Calories: 780; Cholesterol: 165mg; Total Fat: 44g; Saturated Fat: 18g; Sodium: 1480mg; Total Carbohydrates: 51g; Dietary Fiber: 4g; Total Sugars: 4g; Protein: 46g

Crunchy Falafel Balls

Servings: 8 | Prep Time: 15 Minutes | Cooking Time: 16 Minutes

Ingredients:

- 600 grams Drained and rinsed canned chickpeas
- 60 grams Olive oil
- 3 tablespoons All-purpose flour
- 1½ teaspoons Dried oregano
- 1½ teaspoons Dried sage leaves
- 1½ teaspoons Dried thyme
- ¾ teaspoon Table salt
- Olive oil spray

Directions:

1. Preheat the air fryer to 200°C/400°F.
2. Place the chickpeas, olive oil, flour, oregano, sage, thyme, and salt in a food processor. Cover and process into a paste, stopping the machine at least once to scrape down the inside of the canister.
3. Scrape down and remove the blade. Using clean, wet hands, form 2 tablespoons of the paste into a ball, then continue making 9 more balls for a small batch, 15 more for a medium one, and 19 more for a large batch. Generously coat the balls in olive oil spray.
4. Set the balls in the basket in one layer with a little space between them and air-fry undisturbed for 16 minutes, or until well browned and crisp.
5. Dump the contents of the basket onto a wire rack. Cool for 5 minutes before serving.

Variations & Ingredients Tips:

- Add minced garlic, onion, or herbs like parsley or cilantro for extra flavor.
- Serve with tahini sauce, hummus, or tzatziki for dipping.
- Make a falafel sandwich by stuffing pita bread with falafel balls, lettuce, tomato, and sauce.

Per Serving (2 falafel balls): Calories: 170; Cholesterol: 0mg; Total Fat: 9g; Saturated Fat: 1g; Sodium: 230mg; Total Carbohydrates: 18g; Dietary Fiber: 4g; Total Sugars: 2g; Protein: 5g

Chicken Spiedies

Servings: 3 | Prep Time: 15 Minutes (plus Marinating Time) | Cooking Time: 12 Minutes

Ingredients:

- 570 grams Boneless skinless chicken thighs, trimmed of any fat blobs and cut into 5-cm pieces
- 3 tablespoons Red wine vinegar
- 2 tablespoons Olive oil
- 2 tablespoons Minced fresh mint leaves
- 2 tablespoons Minced fresh parsley leaves
- 2 teaspoons Minced fresh dill fronds
- ¾ teaspoon Fennel seeds
- ¾ teaspoon Table salt
- Up to a ¼ teaspoon Red pepper flakes
- 3 Long soft rolls, such as hero, hoagie, or Italian sub rolls (gluten-free, if a concern), split open lengthwise
- 4½ tablespoons Regular or low-fat mayonnaise (not fat-free; gluten-free, if a concern)
- 1½ tablespoons Distilled white vinegar
- 1½ teaspoons Ground black pepper

Directions:

1. Mix the chicken, vinegar, oil, mint, parsley, dill, fennel

seeds, salt, and red pepper flakes in a zip-closed plastic bag. Seal, gently massage the marinade ingredients into the meat, and refrigerate for at least 2 hours or up to 6 hours. (Longer than that and the meat can turn rubbery.)
2. Set the plastic bag out on the counter (to make the contents a little less frigid). Preheat the air fryer to 200°C/400°F.
3. When the machine is at temperature, use kitchen tongs to set the chicken thighs in the basket (discard any remaining marinade) and air-fry undisturbed for 6 minutes. Turn the thighs over and continue air-frying undisturbed for 6 minutes more, until well browned, cooked through, and even a little crunchy.
4. Dump the contents of the basket onto a wire rack and cool for 2 or 3 minutes. Divide the chicken evenly between the rolls. Whisk the mayonnaise, vinegar, and black pepper in a small bowl until smooth. Drizzle this sauce over the chicken pieces in the rolls.

Variations & Ingredients Tips:

- Use chicken breast instead of thighs for a leaner option.
- Substitute the herbs with your favorite combination, such as basil, oregano, or thyme.
- Add sliced onions or pickled vegetables for extra crunch and tanginess.

Per Serving: Calories: 710; Cholesterol: 200mg; Total Fat: 44g; Saturated Fat: 8g; Sodium: 1240mg; Total Carbohydrates: 37g; Dietary Fiber: 2g; Total Sugars: 4g; Protein: 45g

Lamb Burgers

Servings: 3 | Prep Time: 15 Minutes | Cooking Time: 17 Minutes

Ingredients:

- 510 grams Ground lamb
- 3 tablespoons Crumbled feta
- 1 teaspoon Minced garlic
- 1 teaspoon Tomato paste
- ¾ teaspoon Ground coriander
- ¾ teaspoon Ground dried ginger
- Up to ⅛ teaspoon Cayenne
- Up to a ⅛ teaspoon Table salt (optional)
- 3 Kaiser rolls or hamburger buns (gluten-free, if a concern), split open

Directions:

1. Preheat the air fryer to 190°C/375°F.
2. Gently mix the ground lamb, feta, garlic, tomato paste, coriander, ginger, cayenne, and salt (if using) in a bowl until well combined, trying to keep the bits of cheese intact. Form this mixture into two 15-cm patties for the small batch, three 12.5-cm patties for the medium, or four 12.5-cm patties for the large.
3. Set the patties in the basket in one layer and air-fry undisturbed for 16 minutes, or until an instant-read meat thermometer inserted into one burger registers 70°C/160°F. (The cheese is not an issue with the temperature probe in this recipe as it was for the Inside-Out Cheeseburgers, because the feta is so well mixed into the ground meat.)
4. Use a nonstick-safe spatula, and perhaps a flatware fork for balance, to transfer the burgers to a cutting board. Set the buns cut side down in the basket in one layer (working in batches as necessary) and air-fry undisturbed for 1 minute, to toast a bit and warm up. Serve the burgers warm in the buns.

Variations & Ingredients Tips:

- Substitute feta with goat cheese or crumbled blue cheese for a different flavor profile.
- Add finely chopped mint or parsley to the lamb mixture for a fresh, herbal taste.
- Serve with tzatziki sauce, sliced cucumbers, and red onions for a Greek-inspired burger.

Per Serving (1 burger): Calories: 560; Cholesterol: 140mg; Total Fat: 34g; Saturated Fat: 15g; Sodium: 580mg; Total Carbohydrates: 25g; Dietary Fiber: 1g; Total Sugars: 3g; Protein: 38g

Sausage And Pepper Heros

Servings: 3 | Prep Time: 10 Minutes | Cooking Time: 11 Minutes

Ingredients:

- 3 links (about 255 grams total) Sweet Italian sausages (gluten-free, if a concern)
- 1½ Medium red or green bell pepper(s), stemmed, cored, and cut into 1.25-cm-wide strips
- 1 medium Yellow or white onion(s), peeled, halved, and sliced into thin half-moons
- 3 Long soft rolls, such as hero, hoagie, or Italian sub rolls (gluten-free, if a concern), split open lengthwise
- For garnishing Balsamic vinegar

- For garnishing Fresh basil leaves

Directions:

1. Preheat the air fryer to 200°C/400°F.
2. When the machine is at temperature, set the sausage links in the basket in one layer and air-fry undisturbed for 5 minutes.
3. Add the pepper strips and onions. Continue air-frying, tossing and rearranging everything about once every minute, for 5 minutes, or until the sausages are browned and an instant-read meat thermometer inserted into one of the links registers 70°C/160°F.
4. Use a nonstick-safe spatula and kitchen tongs to transfer the sausages and vegetables to a cutting board. Set the rolls cut side down in the basket in one layer (working in batches as necessary) and air-fry undisturbed for 1 minute, to toast the rolls a bit and warm them up. Set 1 sausage with some pepper strips and onions in each warm roll, sprinkle balsamic vinegar over the sandwich fillings, and garnish with basil leaves.

Variations & Ingredients Tips:

- Use hot Italian sausage or chorizo for a spicier sandwich.
- Add sliced mushrooms or zucchini to the pepper and onion mixture for extra veggies.
- Top with shredded mozzarella or provolone cheese for a cheesy twist.

Per Serving (1 sandwich): Calories: 560; Cholesterol: 60mg; Total Fat: 36g; Saturated Fat: 12g; Sodium: 1420mg; Total Carbohydrates: 39g; Dietary Fiber: 3g; Total Sugars: 7g; Protein: 24g

Asian Glazed Meatballs

Servings: 4 | Prep Time: 15 Minutes | Cooking Time: 10 Minutes

Ingredients:

- 1 large shallot, finely chopped
- 2 cloves garlic, minced
- 1 tablespoon grated fresh ginger
- 2 teaspoons fresh thyme, finely chopped
- 1½ cups brown mushrooms, very finely chopped (a food processor works well here)
- 2 tablespoons soy sauce
- freshly ground black pepper
- ½ kg ground beef
- ¼ kg ground pork
- 3 egg yolks
- 1 cup Thai sweet chili sauce (spring roll sauce)
- ¼ cup toasted sesame seeds
- 2 scallions, sliced

Directions:

1. Combine the shallot, garlic, ginger, thyme, mushrooms, soy sauce, freshly ground black pepper, ground beef and pork, and egg yolks in a bowl and mix the ingredients together. Gently shape the mixture into 24 balls, about the size of a golf ball.
2. Preheat the air fryer to 190°C/380°F.
3. Working in batches, air-fry the meatballs for 8 minutes, turning the meatballs over halfway through the cooking time. Drizzle some of the Thai sweet chili sauce on top of each meatball and return the basket to the air fryer, air-frying for another 2 minutes. Reserve the remaining Thai sweet chili sauce for serving.
4. As soon as the meatballs are done, sprinkle with toasted sesame seeds and transfer them to a serving platter. Scatter the scallions around and serve warm.

Variations & Ingredients Tips:

- Use a food processor to finely chop the mushrooms for better texture in the meatballs.
- Work in batches when air frying the meatballs to ensure even cooking and browning.
- Drizzle the Thai sweet chili sauce over the meatballs towards the end of cooking for a nice glaze.

Per Serving: Calories: 550; Cholesterol: 205mg; Total Fat: 32g; Saturated Fat: 11g; Sodium: 1300mg; Total Carbohydrates: 36g; Dietary Fiber: 2g; Total Sugars: 23g; Protein: 29g

Chicken Saltimbocca Sandwiches

Servings: 3 | Prep Time: 10 Minutes | Cooking Time: 11 Minutes

Ingredients:

- 3 140to 170-gram boneless skinless chicken breasts
- 6 Thin prosciutto slices
- 6 Provolone cheese slices
- 3 Long soft rolls, such as hero, hoagie, or Italian sub rolls (gluten-free, if a concern), split open lengthwise
- 3 tablespoons Pesto, purchased or homemade

(see the headnote)

Directions:

1. Preheat the air fryer to 200°C/400°F.
2. Wrap each chicken breast with 2 prosciutto slices, spiraling the prosciutto around the breast and overlapping the slices a bit to cover the breast. The prosciutto will stick to the chicken more readily than bacon does.
3. When the machine is at temperature, set the wrapped chicken breasts in the basket and air-fry undisturbed for 10 minutes, or until the prosciutto is frizzled and the chicken is cooked through.
4. Overlap 2 cheese slices on each breast. Air-fry undisturbed for 1 minute, or until melted. Take the basket out of the machine.
5. Smear the insides of the rolls with the pesto, then use kitchen tongs to put a wrapped and cheesy chicken breast in each roll.

Variations & Ingredients Tips:

- Use fresh mozzarella instead of provolone for a creamier texture.
- Add sliced tomatoes or roasted red peppers for extra flavor and nutrition.
- Substitute prosciutto with ham or bacon if desired.

Per Serving: Calories: 630; Cholesterol: 125mg; Total Fat: 32g; Saturated Fat: 11g; Sodium: 1580mg; Total Carbohydrates: 38g; Dietary Fiber: 2g; Total Sugars: 4g; Protein: 48g

Inside-out Cheeseburgers

Servings: 3 | Prep Time: 15 Minutes | Cooking Time: 9-11 Minutes

Ingredients:

- 510 grams 90% lean ground beef
- ¾ teaspoon Dried oregano
- ¾ teaspoon Table salt
- ¾ teaspoon Ground black pepper
- ¼ teaspoon Garlic powder
- 6 tablespoons (about 45 grams) Shredded Cheddar, Swiss, or other semi-firm cheese, or a purchased blend of shredded cheeses
- 3 Hamburger buns (gluten-free, if a concern), split open

Directions:

1. Preheat the air fryer to 190°C/375°F.
2. Gently mix the ground beef, oregano, salt, pepper, and garlic powder in a bowl until well combined without turning the mixture to mush. Form it into two 15-cm patties for the small batch, three for the medium, or four for the large.
3. Place 2 tablespoons of the shredded cheese in the center of each patty. With clean hands, fold the sides of the patty up to cover the cheese, then pick it up and roll it gently into a ball to seal the cheese inside. Gently press it back into a 12.5-cm burger without letting any cheese squish out. Continue filling and preparing more burgers, as needed.
4. Place the burgers in the basket in one layer and air-fry undisturbed for 8 minutes for medium or 10 minutes for well-done. (An instant-read meat thermometer won't work for these burgers because it will hit the mostly melted cheese inside and offer a hotter temperature than the surrounding meat.)
5. Use a nonstick-safe spatula, and perhaps a flatware fork for balance, to transfer the burgers to a cutting board. Set the buns cut side down in the basket in one layer (working in batches as necessary) and air-fry undisturbed for 1 minute, to toast a bit and warm up. Cool the burgers a few minutes more, then serve them warm in the buns.

Variations & Ingredients Tips:

- Mix different types of cheese like cheddar, mozzarella, and blue cheese for a flavorful combination.
- Add finely chopped bacon or caramelized onions to the cheese stuffing for extra richness.
- Serve with your favorite burger toppings like lettuce, tomato, onion, and pickles.

Per Serving (1 burger): Calories: 480; Cholesterol: 125mg; Total Fat: 27g; Saturated Fat: 11g; Sodium: 720mg; Total Carbohydrates: 22g; Dietary Fiber: 1g; Total Sugars: 3g; Protein: 38g

Inside Out Cheeseburgers

Servings: 2 | Prep Time: 15 Minutes | Cooking Time: 20 Minutes

Ingredients:

- 340 grams lean ground beef
- 3 tablespoons minced onion
- 4 teaspoons ketchup
- 2 teaspoons yellow mustard
- salt and freshly ground black pepper
- 4 slices of Cheddar cheese, broken into smaller pieces

- 8 hamburger dill pickle chips

Directions:

1. Combine the ground beef, minced onion, ketchup, mustard, salt and pepper in a large bowl. Mix well to thoroughly combine the ingredients. Divide the meat into four equal portions.
2. To make the stuffed burgers, flatten each portion of meat into a thin patty. Place 4 pickle chips and half of the cheese onto the center of two of the patties, leaving a rim around the edge of the patty exposed. Place the remaining two patties on top of the first and press the meat together firmly, sealing the edges tightly. With the burgers on a flat surface, press the sides of the burger with the palm of your hand to create a straight edge. This will help keep the stuffing inside the burger while it cooks.
3. Preheat the air fryer to 190°C/370°F.
4. Place the burgers inside the air fryer basket and air-fry for 20 minutes, flipping the burgers over halfway through the cooking time.
5. Serve the cheeseburgers on buns with lettuce and tomato.

Variations & Ingredients Tips:

- Use different types of cheese like Swiss, pepper jack, or blue cheese for a unique flavor.
- Add crispy bacon pieces or sautéed mushrooms to the stuffing for extra richness.
- Brush the burgers with a mixture of melted butter and minced garlic before cooking for added flavor.

Per Serving (1 burger): Calories: 510; Cholesterol: 145mg; Total Fat: 32g; Saturated Fat: 14g; Sodium: 780mg; Total Carbohydrates: 12g; Dietary Fiber: 1g; Total Sugars: 6g; Protein: 42g

Salmon Burgers

Servings: 3 | Prep Time: 15 Minutes | Cooking Time: 8 Minutes

Ingredients:

- 510 grams Skinless salmon fillet, preferably fattier Atlantic salmon
- 1½ tablespoons Minced chives or the green part of a scallion
- ½ cup Plain panko bread crumbs (gluten-free, if a concern)
- 1½ teaspoons Dijon mustard (gluten-free, if a concern)
- 1½ teaspoons Drained and rinsed capers, minced
- 1½ teaspoons Lemon juice
- ¼ teaspoon Table salt
- ¼ teaspoon Ground black pepper
- Vegetable oil spray

Directions:

1. Preheat the air fryer to 190°C/375°F.
2. Cut the salmon into pieces that will fit in a food processor. Cover and pulse until coarsely chopped. Add the chives and pulse to combine, until the fish is ground but not a paste. Scrape down and remove the blade. Scrape the salmon mixture into a bowl. Add the bread crumbs, mustard, capers, lemon juice, salt, and pepper. Stir gently until well combined.
3. Use clean and dry hands to form the mixture into two 12.5-cm patties for a small batch, three 12.5-cm patties for a medium batch, or four 12.5-cm patties for a large one.
4. Coat both sides of each patty with vegetable oil spray. Set them in the basket in one layer and air-fry undisturbed for 8 minutes, or until browned and an instant-read meat thermometer inserted into the center of a burger registers 65°C/145°F.
5. Use a nonstick-safe spatula, and perhaps a flatware fork for balance, to transfer the burgers to a wire rack. Cool for 2 or 3 minutes before serving.

Variations & Ingredients Tips:

- Substitute salmon with canned or leftover cooked salmon for convenience.
- Add finely chopped red bell pepper or celery to the burger mixture for extra crunch and flavor.
- Serve on toasted buns with lettuce, tomato, and a dollop of tartar sauce or remoulade.

Per Serving (1 burger): Calories: 320; Cholesterol: 95mg; Total Fat: 16g; Saturated Fat: 3g; Sodium: 440mg; Total Carbohydrates: 15g; Dietary Fiber: 1g; Total Sugars: 1g; Protein: 31g

Dijon Thyme Burgers

Servings: 3 | Prep Time: 15 Minutes | Cooking Time: 18 Minutes

Ingredients:

- 450 grams lean ground beef
- ⅓ cup panko breadcrumbs
- ¼ cup finely chopped onion

- 3 tablespoons Dijon mustard
- 1 tablespoon chopped fresh thyme
- 4 teaspoons Worcestershire sauce
- 1 teaspoon salt
- freshly ground black pepper
- Topping (optional):
- 2 tablespoons Dijon mustard
- 1 tablespoon dark brown sugar
- 1 teaspoon Worcestershire sauce
- 115 grams sliced Swiss cheese, optional

Directions:

1. Combine all the burger ingredients together in a large bowl and mix well. Divide the meat into 4 equal portions and then form the burgers, being careful not to over-handle the meat. One good way to do this is to throw the meat back and forth from one hand to another, packing the meat each time you catch it. Flatten the balls into patties, making an indentation in the center of each patty with your thumb (this will help it stay flat as it cooks) and flattening the sides of the burgers so that they will fit nicely into the air fryer basket.
2. Preheat the air fryer to 190°C/370°F.
3. If you don't have room for all four burgers, air-fry two or three burgers at a time for 8 minutes. Flip the burgers over and air-fry for another 6 minutes.
4. While the burgers are cooking combine the Dijon mustard, dark brown sugar, and Worcestershire sauce in a small bowl and mix well. This optional topping to the burgers really adds a boost of flavor at the end. Spread the Dijon topping evenly on each burger. If you cooked the burgers in batches, return the first batch to the cooker at this time – it's ok to place the fourth burger on top of the others in the center of the basket. Air-fry the burgers for another 3 minutes.
5. Finally, if desired, top each burger with a slice of Swiss cheese. Lower the air fryer temperature to 165°C/330°F and air-fry for another minute to melt the cheese. Serve the burgers on toasted brioche buns, dressed the way you like them.

Variations & Ingredients Tips:

- Use ground turkey or chicken for a leaner burger option.
- Add minced garlic or finely chopped herbs like parsley or chives for extra flavor.
- Substitute panko breadcrumbs with regular breadcrumbs or oats for a different texture.

Per Serving (1 burger with cheese): Calories: 500; Cholesterol: 120mg; Total Fat: 27g; Saturated Fat: 11g; Sodium: 1180mg; Total Carbohydrates: 21g; Dietary Fi-

ber: 1g; Total Sugars: 5g; Protein: 41g

Chili Cheese Dogs

Servings: 3 | Prep Time: 10 Minutes | Cooking Time: 12 Minutes

Ingredients:

- 340 grams Lean ground beef
- 1½ tablespoons Chile powder
- 240 grams plus 2 tablespoons Jarred sofrito
- 3 Hot dogs (gluten-free, if a concern)
- 3 Hot dog buns (gluten-free, if a concern), split open lengthwise
- 3 tablespoons Finely chopped scallion
- 60 grams Shredded Cheddar cheese

Directions:

1. Crumble the ground beef into a medium or large saucepan set over medium heat. Brown well, stirring often to break up the clumps. Add the chile powder and cook for 30 seconds, stirring the whole time. Stir in the sofrito and bring to a simmer. Reduce the heat to low and simmer, stirring occasionally, for 5 minutes. Keep warm.
2. Preheat the air fryer to 200°C/400°F.
3. When the machine is at temperature, put the hot dogs in the basket and air-fry undisturbed for 10 minutes, or until the hot dogs are bubbling and blistered, even a little crisp.
4. Use kitchen tongs to put the hot dogs in the buns. Top each with about 120 grams of the ground beef mixture, 1 tablespoon of the minced scallion, and 20 grams of the cheese. (The scallion should go under the cheese so it superheats and wilts a bit.) Set the filled hot dog buns in the basket and air-fry undisturbed for 2 minutes, or until the cheese has melted.
5. Remove the basket from the machine. Cool the chili cheese dogs in the basket for 5 minutes before serving.

Variations & Ingredients Tips:

- Use turkey or veggie hot dogs for a healthier option.
- Substitute cheddar cheese with your favorite melty cheese, such as pepper jack or Swiss.
- Add diced onions or jalapeños to the chili for extra flavor and heat.

Per Serving: Calories: 580; Cholesterol: 110mg; Total Fat: 32g; Saturated Fat: 13g; Sodium: 1420mg; Total Carbohydrates: 36g; Dietary Fiber: 5g; Total Sugars: 6g;

Protein: 38g

tein: 45g

Chicken Apple Brie Melt

Servings: 3 | Prep Time: 10 Minutes | Cooking Time: 13 Minutes

Ingredients:

- 3 140 to 170-gram boneless skinless chicken breasts
- Vegetable oil spray
- 1½ teaspoons Dried herbes de Provence
- 85 grams Brie, rind removed, thinly sliced
- 6 Thin cored apple slices
- 3 French rolls (gluten-free, if a concern)
- 2 tablespoons Dijon mustard (gluten-free, if a concern)

Directions:

1. Preheat the air fryer to 190°C/375°F.
2. Lightly coat all sides of the chicken breasts with vegetable oil spray. Sprinkle the breasts evenly with the herbes de Provence.
3. When the machine is at temperature, set the breasts in the basket and air-fry undisturbed for 10 minutes.
4. Top the chicken breasts with the apple slices, then the cheese. Air-fry undisturbed for 2 minutes, or until the cheese is melty and bubbling.
5. Use a nonstick-safe spatula and kitchen tongs, for balance, to transfer the breasts to a cutting board. Set the rolls in the basket and air-fry for 1 minute to warm through. (Putting them in the machine without splitting them keeps the insides very soft while the outside gets a little crunchy.)
6. Transfer the rolls to the cutting board. Split them open lengthwise, then spread 1 teaspoon mustard on each cut side. Set a prepared chicken breast on the bottom of a roll and close with its top, repeating as necessary to make additional sandwiches. Serve warm.

Variations & Ingredients Tips:

- Substitute the Brie with Camembert or another soft cheese of your choice.
- Use pears instead of apples for a different flavor profile.
- Add baby spinach or arugula for extra greens and nutrition.

Per Serving: Calories: 510; Cholesterol: 135mg; Total Fat: 19g; Saturated Fat: 8g; Sodium: 670mg; Total Carbohydrates: 41g; Dietary Fiber: 2g; Total Sugars: 6g; Pro-

Black Bean Veggie Burgers

Servings: 3 | Prep Time: 15 Minutes | Cooking Time: 10 Minutes

Ingredients:

- 1 cup Drained and rinsed canned black beans
- ⅓ cup Pecan pieces
- ⅓ cup Rolled oats (not quick-cooking or steel-cut; gluten-free, if a concern)
- 2 tablespoons (or 1 small egg) Pasteurized egg substitute, such as Egg Beaters (gluten-free, if a concern)
- 2 teaspoons Red ketchup-like chili sauce, such as Heinz
- ¼ teaspoon Ground cumin
- ¼ teaspoon Dried oregano
- ¼ teaspoon Table salt
- ¼ teaspoon Ground black pepper
- Olive oil
- Olive oil spray

Directions:

1. Preheat the air fryer to 200°C/400°F.
2. Put the beans, pecans, oats, egg substitute or egg, chili sauce, cumin, oregano, salt, and pepper in a food processor. Cover and process to a coarse paste that will hold its shape like sugar-cookie dough, adding olive oil in 1-teaspoon increments to get the mixture to blend smoothly. The amount of olive oil is actually dependent on the internal moisture content of the beans and the oats. Figure on about 1 tablespoon (three 1-teaspoon additions) for the smaller batch, with proportional increases for the other batches. A little too much olive oil can't hurt, but a dry paste will fall apart as it cooks and a far-too-wet paste will stick to the basket.
3. Scrape down and remove the blade. Using clean, wet hands, form the paste into two 10 cm patties for the small batch, three 10 cm patties for the medium, or four 10 cm patties for the large batch, setting them one by one on a cutting board. Generously coat both sides of the patties with olive oil spray.
4. Set them in the basket in one layer. Air-fry undisturbed for 10 minutes, or until lightly browned and crisp at the edges.
5. Use a nonstick-safe spatula, and perhaps a flatware fork for balance, to transfer the burgers to a wire rack.

83

Cool for 5 minutes before serving.

Variations & Ingredients Tips:

- Add finely chopped vegetables like bell peppers, onions, or carrots for extra flavor and nutrition.
- Experiment with different spices and herbs, such as smoked paprika, garlic powder, or cilantro.
- For a gluten-free version, ensure all ingredients are certified gluten-free.

Per Serving: Calories: 280; Cholesterol: 0mg; Total Fat: 15g; Saturated Fat: 2g; Sodium: 420mg; Total Carbohydrates: 28g; Dietary Fiber: 8g; Total Sugars: 2g; Protein: 10g

White Bean Veggie Burgers

Servings: 3 | Prep Time: 15 Minutes | Cooking Time: 13 Minutes

Ingredients:

- 320 grams Drained and rinsed canned white beans
- 3 tablespoons Rolled oats (not quick-cooking or steel-cut; gluten-free, if a concern)
- 3 tablespoons Chopped walnuts
- 2 teaspoons Olive oil
- 2 teaspoons Lemon juice
- 1½ teaspoons Dijon mustard (gluten-free, if a concern)
- ¾ teaspoon Dried sage leaves
- ¼ teaspoon Table salt
- Olive oil spray
- 3 Whole-wheat buns or gluten-free whole-grain buns (if a concern), split open

Directions:

1. Preheat the air fryer to 200°C/400°F.
2. Place the beans, oats, walnuts, oil, lemon juice, mustard, sage, and salt in a food processor. Cover and process to make a coarse paste that will hold its shape, about like wet sugar-cookie dough, stopping the machine to scrape down the inside of the canister at least once.
3. Scrape down and remove the blade. With clean and wet hands, form the bean paste into two 10-cm patties for the small batch, three 10-cm patties for the medium, or four 10-cm patties for the large batch. Generously coat the patties on both sides with olive oil spray.
4. Set them in the basket with some space between them and air-fry undisturbed for 12 minutes, or until lightly brown and crisp at the edges. The tops of the burgers will feel firm to the touch.
5. Use a nonstick-safe spatula, and perhaps a flatware fork for balance, to transfer the burgers to a cutting board. Set the buns cut side down in the basket in one layer (working in batches as necessary) and air-fry undisturbed for 1 minute, to toast a bit and warm up. Serve the burgers warm in the buns.

Variations & Ingredients Tips:

- Use black beans, chickpeas, or lentils instead of white beans for a different flavor and color.
- Add grated carrots, zucchini, or beets to the burger mixture for extra nutrition and texture.
- Serve with your favorite burger toppings like lettuce, tomato, onion, and pickles.

Per Serving (1 burger): Calories: 350; Cholesterol: 0mg; Total Fat: 13g; Saturated Fat: 1g; Sodium: 520mg; Total Carbohydrates: 48g; Dietary Fiber: 9g; Total Sugars: 4g; Protein: 14g

Chicken Club Sandwiches

Servings: 3 | Prep Time: 15 Minutes | Cooking Time: 15 Minutes

Ingredients:

- 3 140- to 170-gram boneless skinless chicken breasts
- 6 Thick-cut bacon strips (gluten-free, if a concern)
- 3 Long soft rolls, such as hero, hoagie, or Italian sub rolls (gluten-free, if a concern)
- 3 tablespoons Regular, low-fat, or fat-free mayonnaise (gluten-free, if a concern)
- 3 Lettuce leaves, preferably romaine or iceberg
- 6 6-mm-thick tomato slices

Directions:

1. Preheat the air fryer to 190°C/375°F.
2. Wrap each chicken breast with 2 strips of bacon, spiraling the bacon around the meat, slightly overlapping the strips on each revolution. Start the second strip of bacon farther down the breast but on a line with the start of the first strip so they both end at a lined-up point on the chicken breast.
3. When the machine is at temperature, set the wrapped breasts bacon-seam side down in the basket with space between them. Air-fry undisturbed for 12 min-

utes, until the bacon is browned, crisp, and cooked through and an instant-read meat thermometer inserted into the center of a breast registers 75°C/165°F. You may need to add 2 minutes in the air fryer if the temperature is at 70°C/160°F.
4. Use kitchen tongs to transfer the breasts to a wire rack. Split the rolls open lengthwise and set them cut side down in the basket. Air-fry for 1 minute, or until warmed through.
5. Use kitchen tongs to transfer the rolls to a cutting board. Spread 1 tablespoon mayonnaise on the cut side of one half of each roll. Top with a chicken breast, lettuce leaf, and tomato slice. Serve warm.

Variations & Ingredients Tips:

- Use turkey bacon for a lower-fat option.
- Add sliced avocado or pickled onions for extra flavor and texture.
- Toast the rolls before assembling the sandwiches for a crispy texture.

Per Serving: Calories: 640; Cholesterol: 110mg; Total Fat: 34g; Saturated Fat: 9g; Sodium: 1180mg; Total Carbohydrates: 44g; Dietary Fiber: 2g; Total Sugars: 5g; Protein: 42g

Chicken Gyros

Servings: 4 | Prep Time: 10 Minutes (plus Marinating Time) | Cooking Time: 14 Minutes

Ingredients:

- 4 110to 140-gram boneless skinless chicken thighs, trimmed of any fat blobs
- 2 tablespoons Lemon juice
- 2 tablespoons Red wine vinegar
- 2 tablespoons Olive oil
- 2 teaspoons Dried oregano
- 2 teaspoons Minced garlic
- 1 teaspoon Table salt
- 1 teaspoon Ground black pepper
- 4 Pita pockets (gluten-free, if a concern)
- ½ cup Chopped tomatoes
- ½ cup Bottled regular, low-fat, or fat-free ranch dressing (gluten-free, if a concern)

Directions:

1. Mix the thighs, lemon juice, vinegar, oil, oregano, garlic, salt, and pepper in a zip-closed bag. Seal, gently massage the marinade into the meat through the plastic, and refrigerate for at least 2 hours or up to 6 hours. (Longer than that and the meat can turn rubbery.)
2. Set the plastic bag out on the counter (to make the contents a little less frigid). Preheat the air fryer to 190°C/375°F.
3. When the machine is at temperature, use kitchen tongs to place the thighs in the basket in one layer. Discard the marinade. Air-fry the chicken thighs undisturbed for 12 minutes, or until browned and an instant-read meat thermometer inserted into the thickest part of one thigh registers 75°C/165°F. You may need to air-fry the chicken 2 minutes longer if the machine's temperature is 70°C/360°F.
4. Use kitchen tongs to transfer the thighs to a cutting board. Cool for 5 minutes, then set one thigh in each of the pita pockets. Top each with 2 tablespoons chopped tomatoes and 2 tablespoons dressing. Serve warm.

Variations & Ingredients Tips:

- Substitute chicken thighs with chicken breast for a leaner option.
- Add shredded lettuce, sliced onions, or cucumbers for extra crunch and flavor.
- Use homemade tzatziki sauce instead of ranch dressing for a more authentic taste.

Per Serving: Calories: 460; Cholesterol: 95mg; Total Fat: 28g; Saturated Fat: 5g; Sodium: 1070mg; Total Carbohydrates: 29g; Dietary Fiber: 2g; Total Sugars: 4g; Protein: 25g

Desserts And Sweets

Coconut-custard Pie

Servings: 4 | Prep Time: 10 Minutes | Cooking Time: 20 Minutes

Ingredients:

- 1 cup milk
- ¼ cup plus 2 tablespoons sugar
- ¼ cup biscuit baking mix
- 1 teaspoon vanilla
- 2 eggs
- 2 tablespoons melted butter
- cooking spray
- ½ cup shredded, sweetened coconut

Directions:

1. Place all ingredients except coconut in a medium bowl.
2. Using a hand mixer, beat on high speed for 3 minutes.
3. Let sit for 5 minutes.
4. Preheat air fryer to 165°C/330°F.
5. Spray a 15-cm round or 15x15-cm square baking pan with cooking spray and place pan in air fryer basket.
6. Pour filling into pan and sprinkle coconut over top.
7. Cook pie at 165°C/330°F for 20 minutes or until center sets.

Variations & Ingredients Tips:

- Use coconut milk instead of regular milk for a more intense coconut flavor.
- Add a pinch of nutmeg or cinnamon to the filling.
- Serve with a scoop of vanilla ice cream or a dollop of whipped cream.

Per Serving: Calories: 310; Total Fat: 15g; Saturated Fat: 10g; Sodium: 260mg; Total Carbohydrates: 39g; Dietary Fiber: 1g; Total Sugars: 30g; Protein: 6g

Chocolate Soufflés

Servings: 2 | Prep Time: 15 Minutes | Cooking Time: 14 Minutes

Ingredients:

- Butter and sugar for greasing the ramekins
- 85-g semi-sweet chocolate, chopped
- 1/4 cup unsalted butter
- 2 eggs, yolks and whites separated
- 3 tablespoons sugar
- 1/2 teaspoon pure vanilla extract
- 2 tablespoons all-purpose flour
- Powdered sugar, for dusting
- Heavy cream, for serving

Directions:

1. Butter and sugar two 170-g ramekins.
2. Melt chocolate and butter together.
3. Beat egg yolks, then add sugar, vanilla and melted chocolate. Stir in flour.
4. Preheat air fryer to 165°C/330°F.
5. Whip egg whites to soft peaks, then fold into chocolate mixture.
6. Transfer batter to ramekins, leaving 1.3-cm at top.
7. Air fry for 14 minutes until risen and browned on top.
8. Dust with powdered sugar and serve immediately with cream.

Variations & Ingredients Tips:

- Add a splash of liqueur to the batter.
- Top with fresh berries before serving.
- Use ramekins with straight sides for better rise.

Per Serving: Calories: 575; Total Fat: 41g; Saturated Fat: 24g; Sodium: 165mg; Total Carbohydrates: 48g; Dietary Fiber: 3g; Total Sugars: 36g; Protein: 9g

Fluffy Orange Cake

Servings: 6 | Prep Time: 15 Minutes | Cooking Time: 30 Minutes

Ingredients:

- 1/3 cup cornmeal
- 1 ¼ cups flour
- ¾ cup white sugar
- 1 tsp baking soda
- ¼ cup safflower oil

- 1 ¼ cups orange juice
- 1 tsp orange zest
- ¼ cup powdered sugar

Directions:

1. Preheat air fryer to 170°C/340°F.
2. Mix cornmeal, flour, sugar, baking soda, safflower oil, 1 cup of orange juice, and orange zest in a medium bowl. Mix until combined.
3. Pour the batter into a greased baking pan and set into the air fryer. Bake until a toothpick in the center of the cake comes out clean.
4. Remove the cake and place it on a cooling rack. Use the toothpick to make 20 holes in the cake.
5. Meanwhile, combine the rest of the juice with the powdered sugar in a small bowl. Drizzle the glaze over the hot cake and allow it to absorb.
6. Leave to cool completely, then cut into pieces. Serve and enjoy!

Variations & Ingredients Tips:

- Substitute orange juice and zest with lemon or grapefruit for a different citrus flavor.
- Add poppy seeds or shredded coconut to the batter for extra texture.
- Top with candied orange peel or a sprinkle of cinnamon sugar.

Per Serving: Calories: 350; Total Fat: 10g; Saturated Fat: 1g; Sodium: 270mg; Total Carbohydrates: 63g; Dietary Fiber: 2g; Total Sugars: 39g; Protein: 4g

Baked Stuffed Pears

Servings: 4 | Prep Time: 15 Minutes | Cooking Time: 15 Minutes + Cooling Time

Ingredients:

- 4 cored pears, halved
- 1/2 cup chopped cashews
- 1/2 cup dried cranberries
- 1/4 cup agave nectar
- 1/2 stick butter, softened
- 1/2 tsp ground cinnamon
- 1/2 cup apple juice

Directions:

1. Preheat the air fryer to 180°C/350°F.
2. Combine the cashews, cranberries, agave nectar, butter, and cinnamon and mix well.
3. Stuff this mixture into the pears, heaping it up on top.
4. Set the pears in a baking pan and pour the apple juice into the bottom of the pan.
5. Put the pan in the fryer and Bake for 10-12 minutes or until the pears are tender.
6. Let cool before serving.

Variations & Ingredients Tips:

- Use honey or maple syrup instead of agave nectar.
- Add chopped dates or raisins to the stuffing mixture.
- Sprinkle with cinnamon sugar before baking.

Per Serving: Calories: 370; Total Fat: 19g; Saturated Fat: 7g; Sodium: 83mg; Total Carbohydrates: 51g; Dietary Fiber: 7g; Total Sugars: 36g; Protein: 5g

Holiday Peppermint Cake

Servings: 4 | Prep Time: 10 Minutes | Cooking Time: 20 Minutes

Ingredients:

- 1 1/2 cups flour
- 3 eggs
- 1/3 cup molasses
- 1/2 cup olive oil
- 1/2 cup almond milk
- 1/2 tsp vanilla extract
- 1/2 tsp peppermint extract
- 1 tsp baking powder
- 1/2 tsp salt

Directions:

1. Preheat air fryer to 190°C/380°F.
2. Whisk the eggs and molasses until smooth.
3. Slowly mix in olive oil, almond milk, vanilla and peppermint extracts.
4. In another bowl, sift together flour, baking powder and salt.
5. Gradually incorporate dry ingredients into wet ingredients until combined.
6. Pour batter into a greased baking pan and place in air fryer basket.
7. Bake for 12-15 minutes until a toothpick inserted comes out clean.
8. Serve and enjoy!

Variations & Ingredients Tips:

- Use coconut or vegetable oil instead of olive oil.
- Add crushed peppermint candies or chocolate

chips to the batter.
- ▶ Top with peppermint frosting or whipped cream.

Per Serving: Calories: 538; Total Fat: 27g; Saturated Fat: 4g; Sodium: 307mg; Total Carbohydrates: 67g; Dietary Fiber: 2g; Total Sugars: 28g; Protein: 8g

Holiday Pear Crumble

Servings: 4 | Prep Time: 15 Minutes | Cooking Time: 40 Minutes

Ingredients:

- 2 tbsp coconut oil
- 1/4 cup flour
- 1/4 cup demerara sugar
- 1/8 tsp salt
- 2 cups finely chopped pears
- 1/2 tbsp lemon juice
- 3/4 tsp cinnamon

Directions:

1. In a bowl, mix together coconut oil, flour, sugar and salt until crumbly.
2. Preheat air fryer to 160°C/320°F.
3. Stir together pears, 3 tbsp water, lemon juice and cinnamon in a baking pan.
4. Sprinkle chilled topping evenly over the pear mixture.
5. Bake for 30 minutes until pears are softened and topping is crispy.
6. Serve warm.

Variations & Ingredients Tips:

- ▶ Use apples or a mix of fruits instead of just pears.
- ▶ Add oats, nuts or spices like nutmeg to the crumble topping.
- ▶ Drizzle with caramel sauce before serving.

Per Serving: Calories: 233; Total Fat: 9g; Saturated Fat: 5g; Sodium: 58mg; Total Carbohydrates: 38g; Dietary Fiber: 4g; Total Sugars: 23g; Protein: 2g

Vegan Brownie Bites

Servings: 10 | Prep Time: 10 Minutes | Cooking Time: 8 Minutes

Ingredients:

- 2/3 cup walnuts
- 1/3 cup all-purpose flour
- 1/4 cup dark cocoa powder
- 1/3 cup cane sugar
- 1/4 teaspoon salt
- 2 tablespoons vegetable oil
- 1 teaspoon pure vanilla extract
- 1 tablespoon almond milk
- 1 tablespoon powdered sugar

Directions:

1. Preheat the air fryer to 175°C/350°F.
2. To a blender or food processor fitted with a metal blade, add the walnuts, flour, cocoa powder, sugar, and salt. Pulse until smooth, about 30 seconds.
3. Add in the oil, vanilla, and milk and pulse until a dough is formed.
4. Remove the dough and place in a bowl. Form into 10 equal-size bites.
5. Liberally spray the metal trivet in the air fryer basket with olive oil mist. Place the brownie bites into the basket and cook for 8 minutes, or until the outer edges begin to slightly crack.
6. Remove the basket from the air fryer and let cool. Sprinkle the brownie bites with powdered sugar and serve.

Variations & Ingredients Tips:

- ▶ Use other nut varieties like pecans or almonds.
- ▶ Add chocolate chips or dried fruit to the batter.
- ▶ Use oat flour instead of regular flour to make gluten-free.

Per Serving (1 brownie bite): Calories: 110; Total Fat: 7g; Saturated Fat: 1g; Sodium: 50mg; Total Carbs: 12g; Dietary Fiber: 2g; Total Sugars: 6g; Protein: 2g

Greek Pumpkin Cheesecake

Servings: 4 | Prep Time: 15 Minutes | Cooking Time: 35 Minutes + Chilling Time

Ingredients:

- 2 tbsp peanut butter
- ¼ cup oat flour
- ½ cup Greek yogurt
- 2 tbsp sugar
- ¼ cup ricotta cheese
- ¼ cup canned pumpkin
- 1 tbsp vanilla extract
- 2 tbsp cornstarch
- ¼ tsp ground cinnamon

Directions:

1. Preheat air fryer to 160°C/320°F.
2. For the crust: Whisk the peanut butter, oat flour, 1 tbsp of Greek yogurt, and 1 tsp of sugar until you get a dough. Remove the dough onto a small cake pan and press down to get a 1-cm thick crust. Set aside.
3. Mix the ricotta cheese, pumpkin, vanilla extract, cornstarch, cinnamon, ½ cup of Greek yogurt, and 1 tbsp of sugar until smooth.
4. Pour over the crust and Bake for 20 minutes until golden brown.
5. Let cool completely and refrigerate for 1 hour before serving.

Variations & Ingredients Tips:

- Use almond butter or cashew butter instead of peanut butter for a different flavor.
- Add a pinch of nutmeg, ginger, or cloves to the filling for extra warmth.
- Top with a dollop of whipped cream or a sprinkle of chopped pecans.

Per Serving: Calories: 210; Total Fat: 10g; Saturated Fat: 4g; Sodium: 120mg; Total Carbohydrates: 24g; Dietary Fiber: 2g; Total Sugars: 12g; Protein: 8g

Pumpkin Brownies

Servings: 4 | Prep Time: 10 Minutes | Cooking Time: 30 Minutes

Ingredients:

- 1/4 cup canned pumpkin
- 1/2 cup maple syrup
- 2 eggs, beaten
- 1 tbsp vanilla extract
- 1/4 cup tapioca flour
- 1/4 cup flour
- 1/2 tsp baking powder

Directions:

1. Preheat air fryer to 160°C/320°F.
2. Mix the pumpkin, maple syrup, eggs, and vanilla extract in a bowl.
3. Toss in tapioca flour, flour, and baking powder until smooth.
4. Pour the batter into a small round cake pan and Bake for 20 minutes until a toothpick comes out clean.
5. Let cool completely before slicing into 4 brownies. Serve and enjoy!

Variations & Ingredients Tips:

- Add chocolate chips or nuts to the batter.
- Use almond or coconut flour instead of regular flour.
- Top with cream cheese frosting.

Per Serving: Calories: 240; Total Fat: 4g; Saturated Fat: 1g; Cholesterol: 95mg; Sodium: 90mg; Total Carbs: 47g; Dietary Fiber: 2g; Total Sugars: 26g; Protein: 5g

Easy Bread Pudding

Servings: 4 | Prep Time: 15 Minutes | Cooking Time: 25 Minutes

Ingredients:

- 2 cups sandwich bread cubes
- ½ cup pecan pieces
- ½ cup raisins
- 3 eggs
- ¼ cup half-and-half
- ¼ cup dark corn syrup
- 1 tsp vanilla extract
- 2 tbsp bourbon
- 2 tbsp dark brown sugar
- ¼ tsp ground cinnamon
- ½ tsp nutmeg
- ¼ tsp salt

Directions:

1. Preheat air fryer at 165°C/325°F.
2. Spread the bread pieces in a cake pan and layer pecan pieces and raisins over the top.
3. Whisk the eggs, half-and-half, corn syrup, bourbon, vanilla extract, sugar, cinnamon, nutmeg, and salt in a bowl. Pour egg mixture over pecan pieces. Let sit for 10 minutes.
4. Place the cake pan in the air fryer basket and Bake for 15 minutes.
5. Let cool onto a cooling rack for 10 minutes before slicing. Serve immediately.

Variations & Ingredients Tips:

- Use croissants, brioche, or challah bread instead of sandwich bread for a richer pudding.
- Add diced apples, pears, or bananas to the bread mixture.
- Serve with a scoop of vanilla ice cream or a dollop of whipped cream.

Per Serving: Calories: 470; Total Fat: 20g; Saturated

Fat: 4.5g; Sodium: 380mg; Total Carbohydrates: 65g; Dietary Fiber: 3g; Total Sugars: 40g; Protein: 9g

Honey Apple-pear Crisp

Servings: 4 | Prep Time: 10 Minutes | Cooking Time: 25 Minutes

Ingredients:

- 1 peeled apple, chopped
- 2 peeled pears, chopped
- 2 tbsp honey
- 1/2 cup oatmeal
- 1/3 cup flour
- 3 tbsp sugar
- 2 tbsp butter, softened
- 1/2 tsp ground cinnamon

Directions:

1. Preheat air fryer to 190°C/380°F.
2. Combine the apple, pears, and honey in a baking pan.
3. In a bowl, mix oatmeal, flour, sugar, butter and cinnamon until crumbly.
4. Sprinkle crumble topping over the fruit.
5. Bake for 10-12 minutes until golden.
6. Serve hot.

Variations & Ingredients Tips:

▶ Use maple syrup or agave instead of honey.
▶ Add chopped nuts or coconut to the crumble topping.
▶ Top with vanilla ice cream or whipped cream.

Per Serving: Calories: 232; Total Fat: 7g; Saturated Fat: 4g; Sodium: 40mg; Total Carbohydrates: 42g; Dietary Fiber: 4g; Total Sugars: 23g; Protein: 3g

Vanilla Butter Cake

Servings: 6 | Prep Time: 10 Minutes | Cooking Time: 20-24 Minutes

Ingredients:

- 3/4 cup plus 1 tablespoon All-purpose flour
- 1 teaspoon Baking powder
- 1/4 teaspoon Table salt
- 8 tablespoons (1/2 cup/1 stick) Butter, at room temperature
- 1/2 cup Granulated white sugar
- 2 Large eggs
- 2 tablespoons Whole or low-fat milk (not fat-free)
- 3/4 teaspoon Vanilla extract
- Baking spray

Directions:

1. Preheat the air fryer to 165°C/325°F (or 170°C/330°F, if that's the closest setting).
2. Mix the flour, baking powder, and salt in a small bowl until well combined.
3. Using an electric hand mixer at medium speed, beat the butter and sugar in a medium bowl until creamy and smooth, about 3 minutes, occasionally scraping down the inside of the bowl.
4. Beat in the eggs, as well as the white or a yolk as necessary. Beat in the milk and vanilla until smooth. Turn off the beaters and add the flour mixture. Beat at low speed until thick and smooth.
5. Use the baking spray to generously coat the inside of a 15cm round cake pan for a small batch, a 18cm round cake pan for a medium batch, or a 20cm round cake pan for a large batch. Scrape and spread the batter into the pan, smoothing the batter out to an even layer.
6. Set the pan in the basket and air-fry undisturbed for 20 minutes for a 15cm layer, 22 minutes for a 18cm layer, or 24 minutes for a 20cm layer, or until a toothpick or cake tester inserted into the center of the cake comes out clean. Start checking it at the 15-minute mark to know where you are.
7. Use hot pads or silicone baking mitts to transfer the cake pan to a wire rack. Cool for 5 minutes. To unmold, set a cutting board over the baking pan and invert both the board and the pan. Lift the still-warm pan off the cake layer. Set the wire rack on top of the cake layer and invert all of it with the cutting board so that the cake layer is now right side up on the wire rack. Remove the cutting board and continue cooling the cake for at least 10 minutes or to room temperature, about 30 minutes, before slicing into wedges.

Variations & Ingredients Tips:

▶ Add lemon or orange zest to the batter for extra flavor.
▶ Top with a glaze, frosting or fresh fruit.
▶ Use cake flour instead of all-purpose for a more tender crumb.

Per Serving: Calories: 275; Total Fat: 14g; Saturated Fat: 9g; Cholesterol: 80mg; Sodium: 190mg; Total Carbs: 34g; Dietary Fiber: 1g; Total Sugars: 16g; Protein: 4g

Blueberry Crisp

Servings: 6 | Prep Time: 10 Minutes | Cooking Time: 13 Minutes

Ingredients:

- 3 cups Fresh or thawed frozen blueberries
- 1/3 cup Granulated white sugar
- 1 tablespoon Instant tapioca
- 1/3 cup All-purpose flour
- 1/3 cup Rolled oats (not quick-cooking or steel-cut)
- 1/3 cup Chopped walnuts or pecans
- 1/3 cup Packed light brown sugar
- 5 tablespoons plus 1 teaspoon (2/3 stick) Butter, melted and cooled
- 3/4 teaspoon Ground cinnamon
- 1/4 teaspoon Table salt

Directions:

1. Preheat the air fryer to 200°C/400°F.
2. Mix the blueberries, granulated sugar, and instant tapioca in a 15cm, 18cm or 20cm round cake pan.
3. Set the pan in the basket and air-fry for 5 minutes, until blueberries begin to bubble.
4. Meanwhile, mix flour, oats, nuts, brown sugar, butter, cinnamon, and salt in a bowl.
5. When blueberries bubble, crumble flour mixture evenly on top.
6. Continue air-frying for 8 minutes until topping is browned and filling is bubbling.
7. Transfer pan to a wire rack and cool at least 10 minutes before serving.

Variations & Ingredients Tips:

- Use other berries like raspberries or blackberries.
- Add lemon or orange zest to the crisp topping.
- Serve warm with a scoop of vanilla ice cream.

Per Serving: Calories: 322; Total Fat: 15g; Saturated Fat: 6g; Sodium: 122mg; Total Carbohydrates: 45g; Dietary Fiber: 3g; Total Sugars: 25g; Protein: 4g

Fruit Turnovers

Servings: 6 | Prep Time: 15 Minutes | Cooking Time: 25 Minutes

Ingredients:

- 1 sheet puff pastry dough
- 6 tsp peach preserves
- 3 kiwi, sliced
- 1 large egg, beaten
- 1 tbsp icing sugar

Directions:

1. Prepare puff pastry by cutting it into 6 rectangles. Roll out the pastry with a rolling pin into 13-cm squares. On your workspace, position one square so that it looks like a diamond with points to the top and bottom.
2. Spoon 1 tsp of the preserves on the bottom half and spread it, leaving a 1-cm border from the edge. Place half of one kiwi on top of the preserves. Brush the clean edges with the egg, then fold the top corner over the filling to make a triangle. Crimp with a fork to seal the pastry. Brush the top of the pastry with egg.
3. Preheat air fryer to 180°C/350°F.
4. Put the pastries in the greased air fryer basket. Air Fry for 10 minutes, flipping once until golden and puffy.
5. Remove from the fryer, let cool and dust with icing sugar. Serve.

Variations & Ingredients Tips:

- Use different fruit preserves like strawberry, raspberry, or apricot.
- Substitute kiwi with sliced peaches, plums, or pears.
- Add a sprinkle of cinnamon or nutmeg to the filling for extra flavor.

Per Serving: Calories: 240; Total Fat: 12g; Saturated Fat: 3g; Sodium: 95mg; Total Carbohydrates: 32g; Dietary Fiber: 2g; Total Sugars: 15g; Protein: 4g

Cinnamon Canned Biscuit Donuts

Servings: 4 | Prep Time: 10 Minutes | Cooking Time: 25 Minutes

Ingredients:

- 1 can jumbo biscuits
- 1 cup cinnamon sugar

Directions:

1. Preheat air fryer to 180°C/360°F.
2. Separate biscuits into 8 pieces and cut a hole in the center of each.
3. Place 4 biscuit donuts in the air fryer basket. Spray

with oil.
4. Bake for 8 minutes, flipping once halfway.
5. While still warm, coat donuts in cinnamon sugar mixture.
6. Serve immediately.

Variations & Ingredients Tips:

- Use a glaze or powdered sugar coating instead of cinnamon sugar.
- Fill the centers with fruit jam or chocolate hazelnut spread.
- Drizzle with melted butter before coating in cinnamon sugar.

Per Serving (2 donuts): Calories: 262; Total Fat: 6g; Saturated Fat: 1g; Sodium: 469mg; Total Carbohydrates: 51g; Dietary Fiber: 1g; Total Sugars: 24g; Protein: 4g

Party S'mores

Servings: 6 | Prep Time: 5 Minutes | Cooking Time: 15 Minutes

Ingredients:

- 2 dark chocolate bars, cut into 12 pieces
- 12 buttermilk biscuits
- 12 marshmallows

Directions:

1. Preheat air fryer to 175°C/350°F.
2. Place 6 biscuits in the air fryer. Top each square with a piece of dark chocolate.
3. Bake for 2 minutes. Add a marshmallow to each piece of chocolate.
4. Cook for another minute. Remove and top with another piece of biscuit.
5. Serve warm.

Variations & Ingredients Tips:

- Use graham crackers instead of buttermilk biscuits for a more traditional s'more.
- Substitute dark chocolate with milk chocolate or white chocolate.
- Add a sprinkle of cinnamon or sea salt on top for extra flavor.

Per Serving (2 s'mores): Calories: 280; Total Fat: 12g; Saturated Fat: 6g; Cholesterol: 5mg; Sodium: 370mg; Total Carbs: 40g; Dietary Fiber: 1g; Total Sugars: 18g; Protein: 4g

Cheese & Honey Stuffed Figs

Servings: 4 | Prep Time: 10 Minutes | Cooking Time: 15 Minutes

Ingredients:

- 8 figs, stem off
- 57 grams cottage cheese
- ¼ tsp ground cinnamon
- ¼ tsp orange zest
- ¼ tsp vanilla extract
- 2 tbsp honey
- 1 tbsp olive oil

Directions:

1. Preheat air fryer to 180°C/360°F.
2. Cut an "X" in the top of each fig 1/3 way through, leaving intact the base.
3. Mix together the cottage cheese, cinnamon, orange zest, vanilla extract and 1 tbsp of honey in a bowl.
4. Spoon the cheese mixture into the cavity of each fig.
5. Put the figs in a single layer in the air fryer basket. Drizzle the olive oil over the top of the figs and Roast for 10 minutes.
6. Drizzle with the remaining honey. Serve and enjoy!

Variations & Ingredients Tips:

- Use ricotta, mascarpone, or goat cheese instead of cottage cheese.
- Substitute figs with pitted dates or apricots.
- Sprinkle with chopped pistachios or walnuts before serving.

Per Serving: Calories: 180; Total Fat: 6g; Saturated Fat: 1.5g; Sodium: 85mg; Total Carbohydrates: 30g; Dietary Fiber: 3g; Total Sugars: 26g; Protein: 4g

Chocolate Cake

Servings: 8 | Prep Time: 10 Minutes | Cooking Time: 20 Minutes

Ingredients:

- 1/2 cup sugar
- 1/4 cup flour, plus 3 tablespoons
- 3 tablespoons cocoa
- 1/2 teaspoon baking powder
- 1/2 teaspoon baking soda
- 1/4 teaspoon salt
- 1 egg

- 2 tablespoons oil
- 1/2 cup milk
- 1/2 teaspoon vanilla extract

Directions:

1. Preheat air fryer to 165°C/330°F.
2. Grease and flour a 15x15cm baking pan.
3. In a bowl, stir together sugar, flours, cocoa, baking powder, soda and salt.
4. Add egg, oil, milk and vanilla. Beat with a whisk until smooth.
5. Pour batter into prepared pan.
6. Bake at 330°F for 20 minutes until toothpick inserted comes out clean.

Variations & Ingredients Tips:

- Add chocolate chips or chopped nuts to the batter.
- Substitute buttermilk for a moister cake.
- Top with chocolate frosting or powdered sugar.

Per Serving: Calories: 149; Total Fat: 4g; Saturated Fat: 1g; Sodium: 158mg; Total Carbohydrates: 26g; Dietary Fiber: 1g; Total Sugars: 14g; Protein: 3g

Vanilla Cupcakes With Chocolate Chips

Servings: 2 | Prep Time: 10 Minutes | Cooking Time: 25 Minutes + Cooling Time

Ingredients:

- 1/2 cup white sugar
- 1 1/2 cups flour
- 2 tsp baking powder
- 1/2 tsp salt
- 2/3 cup sunflower oil
- 1 egg
- 2 tsp maple extract
- 1/4 cup vanilla yogurt
- 1 cup chocolate chips

Directions:

1. Preheat air fryer to 175°C/350°F.
2. Combine the sugar, flour, baking powder, and salt in a bowl and stir to combine.
3. Whisk the egg in a separate bowl. Pour in the sunflower oil, yogurt, and maple extract, and continue whisking until light and fluffy.
4. Spoon the wet mixture into the dry ingredients and stir to combine. Gently fold in the chocolate chips with a spatula.
5. Divide the batter between cupcake cups and Bake in the air fryer for 12-15 minutes or until a toothpick comes out dry.
6. Remove the cupcakes let them cool. Serve.

Variations & Ingredients Tips:

- Use other mix-ins like nuts, dried fruit or sprinkles instead of chocolate chips.
- Top with buttercream, cream cheese or glaze frosting.
- Make into a sheet cake instead of cupcakes.

Per Serving (1 cupcake): Calories: 680; Total Fat: 40g; Saturated Fat: 6g; Cholesterol: 35mg; Sodium: 440mg; Total Carbs: 76g; Dietary Fiber: 3g; Total Sugars: 34g; Protein: 7g

Chocolate Macaroons

Servings: 16 | Prep Time: 15 Minutes | Cooking Time: 8 Minutes

Ingredients:

- 2 Large egg whites, at room temperature
- 1/8 teaspoon Table salt
- 1/2 cup Granulated white sugar
- 1 1/2 cups Unsweetened shredded coconut
- 3 tablespoons Unsweetened cocoa powder

Directions:

1. Preheat the air fryer to 190°C/375°F.
2. Beat the egg whites and salt until stiff peaks form.
3. Gradually beat in the sugar until meringue is shiny and thick.
4. Fold in the coconut and cocoa gently until combined.
5. Scoop 2 tbsp portions and roll into balls (16 total).
6. Line air fryer basket with parchment paper and place balls with space between.
7. Air fry for 8 minutes until dry and lightly browned.
8. Transfer to a wire rack and cool at least 10 minutes before serving.

Variations & Ingredients Tips:

- Use sweetened shredded coconut for a sweeter macaroon.
- Add a teaspoon of instant coffee or espresso powder to the cocoa.

▶ Drizzle with melted chocolate after baking.

Per Serving (1 macaroon): Calories: 72; Total Fat: 3g; Saturated Fat: 2g; Sodium: 34mg; Total Carbohydrates: 11g; Dietary Fiber: 1g; Total Sugars: 9g; Protein: 1g

Carrot Cake With Cream Cheese Icing

Servings: 6 | Prep Time: 30 Minutes | Cooking Time: 55 Minutes

Ingredients:

- 1¼ cups all-purpose flour
- 1 teaspoon baking powder
- ½ teaspoon baking soda
- 1 teaspoon ground cinnamon
- ¼ teaspoon ground nutmeg
- ¼ teaspoon salt
- 2 cups grated carrot (about 3 to 4 medium carrots or 2 large)
- ¾ cup granulated sugar
- ¼ cup brown sugar
- 2 eggs
- ¾ cup canola or vegetable oil
- For the icing:
- 227 grams cream cheese, softened at room temperature
- 113 grams butter (110-g or 1 stick), softened at room temperature
- 1 cup powdered sugar
- 1 teaspoon pure vanilla extract

Directions:

1. Grease a 18-cm cake pan.
2. Combine the flour, baking powder, baking soda, cinnamon, nutmeg and salt in a bowl. Add the grated carrots and toss well.
3. In a separate bowl, beat the sugars and eggs together until light and frothy. Drizzle in the oil, beating constantly. Fold the egg mixture into the dry ingredients until everything is just combined and you no longer see any traces of flour.
4. Pour the batter into the cake pan and wrap the pan completely in greased aluminum foil.
5. Preheat the air fryer to 180°C/350°F.
6. Lower the cake pan into the air fryer basket using a sling made of aluminum foil (fold a piece of aluminum foil into a strip about 5-cm wide by 60-cm long). Fold the ends of the aluminum foil into the air fryer, letting them rest on top of the cake. Air-fry for 40 minutes. Remove the aluminum foil cover and air-fry for an additional 15 minutes or until a skewer inserted into the center of the cake comes out clean and the top is nicely browned.
7. While the cake is cooking, beat the cream cheese, butter, powdered sugar and vanilla extract together using a hand mixer, stand mixer or food processor (or a lot of elbow grease!).
8. Remove the cake pan from the air fryer and let the cake cool in the cake pan for 10 minutes or so. Then remove the cake from the pan and let it continue to cool completely.
9. Frost the cake with the cream cheese icing and serve.

Variations & Ingredients Tips:

▶ Add ½ cup of raisins, chopped walnuts, or pecans to the batter.
▶ Substitute ¼ cup of the oil with unsweetened applesauce for a lower fat version.
▶ Use a lemon cream cheese frosting for a tangy twist.

Per Serving: Calories: 740; Total Fat: 49g; Saturated Fat: 20g; Sodium: 470mg; Total Carbohydrates: 71g; Dietary Fiber: 2g; Total Sugars: 49g; Protein: 8g

INDEX

A

Acorn Squash Halves With Maple Butter Glaze	67
Albóndigas	45
Argentinian Steak Asado Salad	42
Asian Glazed Meatballs	79

B

Bacon, Broccoli And Swiss Cheese Bread Pudding	12
Baked Eggs	12
Baked Ricotta With Lemon And Capers	20
Baked Stuffed Pears	87
Balsamic London Broil	44
Basic Fried Tofu	61
Basil Green Beans	64
Beefy Quesadillas	43
Beer-battered Cod	54
Beer-breaded Halibut Fish Tacos	47
Bengali Samosa With Mango Chutney	59
Berry-glazed Turkey Breast	30
Best-ever Roast Beef Sandwiches	75
Black Bean Veggie Burgers	83
Blueberry Crisp	91
Broccoli Cheddar Stuffed Potatoes	61
Broccoli Tots	67
Buttered Brussels Sprouts	74
Buttered Turkey Breasts	33
Butternut Medallions With Honey Butter And Sage	68
Buttery Stuffed Tomatoes	66

C

Californian Tilapia	54
Carrot Cake With Cream Cheese Icing	94
Catfish Nuggets	53
Cheddar Stuffed Portobellos With Salsa	57
Cheddar-bean Flautas	63
Cheese & Honey Stuffed Figs	92

Cheese Wafers	18
Cheesy Potato Canapés With Bacon	22
Cheesy Spinach Dip(2)	22
Cherry-apple Oatmeal Cups	13
Chicken Apple Brie Melt	83
Chicken Club Sandwiches	84
Chicken Cordon Bleu	29
Chicken Flautas	37
Chicken Gyros	85
Chicken Hand Pies	28
Chicken Salad With Sunny Citrus Dressing	67
Chicken Saltimbocca Sandwiches	79
Chicken Spiedies	77
Chicken Strips	31
Chili Cheese Dogs	82
Chili Hash Browns	10
Chinese Fish Noodle Bowls	52
Chinese-style Lamb Chops	44
Chipotle Pork Meatballs	38
Chive Potato Pierogi	56
Chocolate Cake	92
Chocolate Macaroons	93
Chocolate Soufflés	86
Cinnamon Canned Biscuit Donuts	91
Classic Salisbury Steak Burgers	46
Coconut Mini Tarts	10
Coconut-custard Pie	86
Coffee Cake	13
Colorful French Toast Sticks	11
Country Gravy	11
Crispy Five-spice Pork Belly	41
Crispy Wontons	24
Crunchy Falafel Balls	77
Crunchy French Toast Sticks	15
Crunchy Fried Pork Loin Chops	46

D

Delicious Juicy Pork Meatballs	39
Dijon Thyme Burgers	81
Dill Fried Pickles With Light Ranch Dip	19

E

Easy Bread Pudding	89
Easy Tex-mex Chimichangas	40
Easy Turkey Meatballs	30
Eggplant Parmesan Subs	76

F

Falafel	59
Falafels	58
Favorite Blueberry Muffins	16
Filled French Toast	18
Florentine Stuffed Tomatoes	71
Fluffy Orange Cake	86
French Fries	72
Fried Dill Pickle Chips	27
Fried Peaches	23
Fruit Turnovers	91

G

Garlic Parmesan Kale Chips	25
Garlic-cheese Biscuits	17
Garlicky Sea Bass With Root Veggies	49
Goat Cheese, Beet, And Kale Frittata	11
Granola	15
Greek Pork Chops	45
Greek Pumpkin Cheesecake	88
Grilled Cheese Sandwich Deluxe	21
Grits Again	71
Grits Casserole	73
Guajillo Chile Chicken Meatballs	29

H

Hawaiian Chicken	34
Hearty Salad	63
Herbed Baby Red Potato Hasselback	65
Holiday Pear Crumble	88
Holiday Peppermint Cake	87
Homemade French Fries	23
Honey Apple-pear Crisp	90
Honey-mustard Asparagus Puffs	69
Hot Calamari Rings	49

I

Indonesian Pork Satay	40
Inside Out Cheeseburgers	80
Inside-out Cheeseburgers	80
Irresistible Cheesy Chicken Sticks	31
Italian Sausage & Peppers	39
Italian-style Fried Cauliflower	65

K

Kale & Rice Chicken Rolls	31
Kid's Flounder Fingers	54
Kielbasa Chunks With Pineapple & Peppers	40

L

Lamb Burgers	78
Lamb Meatballs With Quick Tomato Sauce	37
Lemon & Herb Crusted Salmon	50
Lentil Burritos With Cilantro Chutney	57
Light Frittata	14
Lovely Mac'n'cheese	66

M

Maple Balsamic Glazed Salmon	55
Mexican Cheeseburgers	76
Mexican Twice Air-fried Sweet Potatoes	63
Mexican-inspired Chicken Breasts	28
Morning Apple Biscuits	12
Morning Potato Cakes	16
Mushroom Bolognese Casserole	58
Mustardy Chicken Bites	29

N

Nacho Chicken Fries	32
Nashville Hot Chicken	33

O

Orange Rolls	16

P

Panko-breaded Cod Fillets	49
Panko-breaded Onion Rings	23
Parmesan Crackers	19
Party Buffalo Chicken Drumettes	35
Party S'mores	92
Peachy Chicken Chunks With Cherries	

Pecorino Dill Muffins	70
Peppered Steak Bites	42
Peppery Tilapia Roulade	55
Perfect Broccoli	72
Perfect Pork Chops	38
Pizza Eggplant Rounds	62
Pizza Margherita With Spinach	59
Pork Tenderloin Salad	69
Pumpkin Bread With Walnuts	14
Pumpkin Brownies	89

Q

Quick-to-make Quesadillas	57

R

Reuben Sandwiches	74
Rich Clam Spread	21
Rich Turkey Burgers	32
Ricotta Veggie Potpie	64
Roasted Corn Salad	73
Roasted Jalapeño Salsa Verde	25

S

Salmon Burgers	81
Salmon Puttanesca En Papillotte With Zucchini	48
Sardinas Fritas	48
Sausage And Pepper Heros	78
Simple Roasted Sweet Potatoes	70
Simple Salsa Chicken Thighs	34
Skinny Fries	26
Spiced Salmon Croquettes	52
Spicy Black Bean Turkey Burgers With Cumin-avocado Spread	36
Spinach And Feta Stuffed Chicken Breasts	35
Sriracha Short Ribs	44
Steamboat Shrimp Salad	68
Strawberry Toast	13
String Bean Fries	21
Stuffed Mushrooms	25
Stunning Apples & Onions	72
Summer Sea Scallops	50
Sweet & Spicy Swordfish Kebabs	53

Sweet-and-salty Pretzels — 19

T

Tender Steak With Salsa Verde — 45

Thai-style Crab Wontons — 26

Thai-style Pork Sliders — 75

The Best Oysters Rockefeller — 51

Tilapia Al Pesto — 50

Timeless Garlic-lemon Scallops — 53

Tortilla Pizza Margherita — 60

Traditional Italian Beef Meatballs — 41

Truffle Vegetable Croquettes — 71

Tuna Nuggets In Hoisin Sauce — 51

V

Vanilla Butter Cake — 90

Vanilla Cupcakes With Chocolate Chips — 93

Vegan Brownie Bites — 88

Vegetarian Stuffed Bell Peppers — 62

W

White Bean Veggie Burgers — 84

Wrapped Smokies In Bacon — 27

Z

Zucchini Hash Browns — 17

Zucchini Tacos — 60